KNOW YOUR PSYCHE

Book Two

Francois Renault

Ideal Publishing
LightPublishing@aol.com

New York, New York
United States of America

First English Edition
F.J. Reynolds©2010

Library of Congress Card Number:
2010929553
International Standard Book Number:
978-0-9621682-7-7

Book 2 of:
Reflective Insights

DEDICATION

To all the great psychologists,
of past, present and future.

OTHER BOOKS
By FRANCOIS RENAULT

CONTENTS

Know Your Psyche

12

INTRODUCTION

YOU ARE MORE

One of the most unique things about human beings is the quality of their intelligence. This being the case, one would think that a standard definition of intelligence would be in place and universally accepted. Yet it has been difficult for researchers to agree on a uniform definition of intelligence, precisely because human consciousness is very unique and hard to pinpoint. Of course, there are other sentient beings sharing the Earth with us who also display high levels of intelligence. If we wish to understand the nature of intelligence, the challenge is first to define the qualities of our own intelligent characteristics and then compare these to those of other highly intelligent beings.

It is hoped that this book will fulfill two objectives:

• to inspire the reader to enhance his or her consciousness,

• to stimulate deeper thought on matters of the mind.

Perhaps the reader will come to understand that each of us is quite cable of investigating the universe with our own mind, for we all have the potential for transforming our consciousness into higher gear. This presentation may serve as one of many stepping stones on the path to that transformation. The reader need not believe anything shared here, for the objective is simply to inspire, to make you aware of your potential. Certainly, no attempt is made to prove anything.

The Human Equation. In ancient Greece, many mystery schools emphasized the commandment, "Man, know thyself!" This decree was inscribed over the doorways to ancient temples, inspiring humans to perfect themselves. Whoever first wrote these immortal words was extremely insightful, realizing that the attainment of wisdom, balance and happiness comes only after we understand ourselves. The statement can also be reworded as, "Know your psyche," for knowing ourselves means knowing our mind. In fact, the term "psyche" has its origins in Greek mythology. It originally referred to a winged girl who was adored by Cupid. This is a powerful analogy, for the human psyche is indeed relatively young and is pursued relentlessly by the heart, which it often ignores.

Whereas elements of the psyche cannot always be proven through scientific means, they can be proven through personal experience. And whereas scientific methods cannot validate all things in Life, personal experience can fill in the blanks. We can and should confirm our own potential without having to wait for the "experts" to do it for us.

The insights shared within this presentation are meant to help the reader delve into his or her psyche. It is important to grasp that we are not merely biological machines — but much more! For one thing, our minds are linked with a universal knowing, and thus we are never alone. Cynicism, on the other hand, severs our connection with this eternal knowing.

In the course of evolution, humanity has inadvertently fragmented its mind, so that it now relies on institutional authority for self validation. However, institutions confirm our worthiness only if we are willing to take their side. That is, they are willing to confirm our worthiness only if we obey their doctrines and support them monetarily. Fortunately, an era is coming when we will be able to celebrate our worthiness without institutional control. Our true selves will eventually burn through all the rubbish that we know as superstition and institutional dogma. As we become familiar with our psyche, we will piece together the fragments of our minds, learning to focus it as a laser. The time has come to start healing our mind and jump our consciousness into higher gear.

Fear and superstition have been the two biggest obstacles to human evolution. Even now, many individuals believe that powers of the psyche are manifestations of evil. However, the real evil is in wasting human potential by giving it away to others. Our higher consciousness has been calling us for eons, inviting us to accept our true spiritual heritage. As we learn to think outside the conventional box, without fear, judgment or confusion, we will rediscover and embrace our divinity. For too long, false doctrines have obscured our worthiness by teaching us blind obedience to external institutions. But external forces are not alone in the blame game. Spiritual laziness also has been part of the false equation that has held us back.

Contrary to erroneous logic, Life is not held

together by chaotic chance. Life is not one gigantic accident! Everything is moved by unseen universal principles, which apply to the psyche as well. Clearly, our consciousness is a dynamic force to reckon with. Yet we have known so little about it. Its full potential is yet to be fully expressed — but it will be in the near future. As our sense of worthiness increases, institutions will have to relinquish their control. They will have to accept the freedom that our minds crave. One by one, in ever-increasing numbers, individuals will be jumping out of their box, releasing themselves from their mental prisons. As they open their minds, they will perceive new insights that do not fit the old paradigm of consciousness. These insights will show us that Life is much grander than we have ever imagined.

It is a fact that, throughout history, there have been individuals who are gifted with special psi (mental) abilities. Although it is difficult to discuss this concept without raising skepticism, it is a phenomenon that continually expresses itself within humanity. One factor that may help understand how psi abilities work is the energy matrix within our bodies. Parapsychological research has long since established that there is definitely an energetic double that envelopes the physical one. In fact, the human body is composed of several energetic bodies. Due to these energy bodies, we are really multi-dimensional beings capable of shifting our awareness from the three-dimensional (3D) world to higher levels of perception. However, because we are focused on the physical world, we often mistakenly believe there is nothing more to reality. Nevertheless, ignorance of other dimensions does not mean they do not exist. The same can be said of psi abilities: just because we may not presently have them does not mean other individuals do not express them.

As humanity continues to evolve, an increasing number of individuals will be able to investigate other dimensional worlds. Furthermore, having psi abilities will help us live more harmonious, balanced lives. Yet, even more than psi abilities, humanity needs to develop a heart-centered consciousness. We have reached an impasse, and only with a receptive heart and clear mind will our consciousness develop beyond its present point.

If the reader is open minded enough, he or she is invited to contemplate the ideas presented within this book. However, any attempt to prove them would simply lead to a "battle of wits" with skeptics. Skeptics tend to prefer building ever-higher walls of resistance, rather than understanding that "proof" is what we allow it to be. On the other hand, there is sound logic in believing in unseen powers and dimensions. To view other dimensional realities, we only need to tune into them.

Of course, in the scientific world skepticism is meant to develop well-disciplined objectivity. Based on this same premise, we should be skeptical of cultural biases as well. We should question all scientific theories and apparent "facts." We must learn to rely on our inner compass to analyze reality. For example, many hard core cynics say, "Show us the soul and prove its existence! Give us the opportunity to touch it, weigh it and test it." Of course, this attitude pre-defines their reality, killing any chance of proving the existence of the soul. The name of their game is: "Deny the unusual!" Skeptics have an astonishing ability to dismiss information that does not conform to their preconceived notions of reality. As long as science insists on proceeding from the known to the unknown, only personal experience will suffice for those who are pathfinders into new realms. It is clear that we should not discern Life by logic alone. We must be willing to put reason aside and observe with our hearts as well.

Believing in psi abilities does not really require a leap of faith. Each of us can learn to trust our inner truth compass; we can develop a personal understanding of our psyche. Furthermore, it is not always necessary to be "objective" about matters of the heart and mind, for the fundamental principles defining extra-sensory perception may never be "proven" in the laboratory. Such proof will come from self exploration of our own abilities.

Like a ripple upon water, an awakening is coming to human consciousness. This awakening will lead to in-roads into the mental realm, because the next major developments will be in the psychic dimension. Mainstream humanity will eventually recognize that our innate psychic capacities are standard operating equipment for everyone in our species – there is nothing supernatural about them!

Although some individuals confuse pessimism with pragmatism, we must expand our consciousness beyond that dumb approach. We can assimilate knowledge of contrasting value, thereby enriching our lives in a practical manner. When humanity becomes fully self-aware in a balanced manner, only then will we become a truly tolerant and enlightened species.

By assuming responsibility as co-creators with Life, we can grow beyond simply re-acting to circumstances; we can become true movers of reality. Otherwise, we are like ships without sails, awaiting currents to push us in new directions. Thus, it is the author's hope that this presentation will encourage the reader to fully embrace his or her own consciousness.

CHAPTER ONE

THE PSI EQUATION

As we embrace our role as co-creators with Life, we should grasp what it means to be a human being — who, what, how and why:

•Who: Most prominently, we have our ego to work with, which is the most basic essence of our psychological being. The ego, which protects the physical self, is the "who" of our present existence and is derived from several base instincts. It is both our strength and our weakness. Because, on the one hand, our egos ground us in reality by discerning all information coming to us so as to maintain some sense of order. Yet the ego will also deny and distort the truth at all costs, if it finds it threatening to its sense of order – no matter how weak its ordered foundation may be. In fact, all individuals hold sets of contradictory views, because the ego is never able to completely consolidate them into a coherent reality.

Human nature is driven by two needs: to be rewarded as well as to avoid punishing situations. Thus the ego (undersoul) is motivated to maintain its sense of security by doing what it considers successful. This need for self-preservation often manifests as a struggle between our lower (animal) instincts and our higher (spiritual) desires to demonstrate altruistic acts. Socially constructive acts are possible because of the ego's "movable boundaries," meaning that our definition of self can be expanded to include the welfare of others. Examples are parents caring for their offspring, friends looking after each other, athletes playing as a team, and comrades demonstrating loyalty to each other. Thus our egos are not simply a selfish essence; they have the capacity to expand to include others within the desire to survive.

For survival the ego relies on the basic instinct of fear. This is why so many (too many) individuals live their lives within the realm of constant fear. Their every decision is based on fear of negative repercussions. Their lives are constantly defined by fear at every decision. True, some fears make self-preservation possible. But constructive fears are based on logic; it is normal to hold such fears as a matter of survival. Unfortunately, many forms of fear simply lead to a vicious circle of self-fulfilling prophecies.

When we base our lives on irrational fears, we feed those fears more energy, thereby attracting the very things we fear. The fears become our reality, and thus we re-enforce the belief that we are smart to live by means of constant fear. But we can release illogical fears that impede our spiritual potential, for they only force us to contract into control dramas.

Needless to say, not all feelings are bad. Emotion of itself is a perfectly normal and desirable quality and must not be confused with feelings of fear. Feeling guilt over expressions of anger or sadness is also a destructive dead-end and will not be productive in the long run. Like the steam pressure building up in a kettle, emotional energy must eventually find an outlet; or the consequences will be explosive.

•What: Most importantly, it is important to underscore that we are a consciousness residing in bodies of an electromagnetic nature. Our vehicles bestow us with a tremendous array of tools with which to wield our willpower upon the world. Do not underestimate the beauty and power inherent within the body temple. Through it many miraculous circumstances have been performed. And you, via your bodily expressions, also create awesome experiences as you journey through your adventures in Life.

Knowing the "what" nature of our spiritual and physical essences helps us understand the troubling disorders often found in many individuals. Many irrational thought patterns resonate from an unbalanced electromagnetic system, expressed as bio-electric short circuits. Once ingrained within the electromagnetic system in the body, it is difficult to undo them, since they reverberate out throughout the whole structure in a domino effect. Thus problematic patterns must be treated in a holistic manner.

Research continues to make tremendous progress towards understanding the basis of bio-chemical and electromagnetic imbalances. Some pioneers continue to pursue research ever deeper into the magnetic causes of many problems, making steady inroads into the workings of electromagnetic forces which affect our mental and physical health.

• How: Although our brains and bodies are obviously of a biological nature, when we delve deeper we perceive an electro-magnetic quality. Medical science has unequivocally demonstrated that:

- the nervous and immune systems are interconnected; and

- bodily systems communicate with each other via electromagnetic signals. This communication is accomplished both directly via the nervous system, as well as indirectly by hormonal impulses. This is the reason why a wide collection of devices have been invented to measure the bio-electrical nature of the body/brain system.

•Why: The "why" of human existence is unquestionably the most difficult for humanity to concede. Religions, sciences and politics have all taken turns at trying to make sense of the human presence. The bottom line is that, born with intelligence and power, humanity has always been accomplishing what it was born to do: create, learn, uplift. As a parent often observes, children will create much havoc in the process of maturing. And only after reaching adulthood are most individuals able to manifest their greatest gifts of assistance to others.

Historically, the same holds true for humanity. As a race of young spiritual entities, we have hated and destroyed in the name of a God which, ironically, we declare all merciful and loving. The savagery that continues today in the world need not be related here, as it is already over exposed by the media. On the other hand, there is little sensationalism in the beauty presented by the enlightened individual. That is why goodness rarely makes it to the front pages of newspapers or magazines.

Thus the individual who wishes to pursue his or her divine worth will not depend on public approval – it simply is not newsworthy! Without fanfare, the spiritual individual will quietly accept his or her responsibility as a co-creator with Life.

Coming to terms as a co-creator is a lifelong project of ever-growing in understanding of Life. Motives, desires and views must be constantly scrutinized for distortion, since corruption seems to be a common thread in all things human.

Our Heritage. Even with our flaws, humanity has been blessed with intrinsic gifts. Parapsychological research has indicated that one in every five individuals has an above normal psychic inclination. Sometimes this inclination is naturally enhanced; sometimes it is accidentally enhanced; and at other times it has been deliberately enhanced.

For example, one well-known psychic acquired his extra-sensory perception (ESP) after receiving eye surgery. Theoretically, his pineal gland was accidentally stimulated during the operation via nerves that link it to the eyes. Thereafter, the subject's psi abilities became pronounced to a remarkable level. Likewise, psi abilities remain dormant within each of us – just waiting to be activated at the appropriate time.

Psi expressions can also be triggered by environmental factors. It has been observed that a receptive, psychic environment tends to generate psychic abilities among its inhabitants. Children raised in a supportive atmosphere of this type tend to develop a higher degree of ESP than those not exposed to psi experiences. But it is not simply a matter of social support but of frequency. Due to the heavy energy in the world, it is difficult for most of us to develop extra-sensory powers. However, the planetary frequency has been gradually speeding up. And with every generation, the Earth's energetic field has been refined ever more.

Lastly, there is often a heredity component at play in regards to psychic ability. There appears to be a gene (or set of genes) that enhances ESP ability. This theory is based on the fact that psychics who are born with psi abilities also tend to have relatives who are equally gifted.

Not only is everyone already partially telepathic, naturally receiving and sending mental signals, but we are all intuitive as well. Intuition is a psi ability that originates in the Superconscious Mind. It is a feeling or sense about something for which we otherwise have no logical knowledge. Since everyone receives intuitive feelings, then everyone is psychic to a degree. Experiments have suggested that psychic senses are similar to the five common senses in that they also function as change detectors.

Types of Psi Abilities. There are at least five types of extra-sensory perception:

• Psychometry is the ability to read frequency patterns that radiate from inanimate objects. Psychics can "feel" the impressions radiating from objects, perceiving specific events emanating from them. Any object can function as a recorder of its surroundings, but quartz crystal is particularly good at preserving energy impressions.

• Precognition refers to the ability to foretell future events. Those who exhibit this sense have proven that the ability is not limited by time or space. This is because the mind is not boxed in by our three-dimensional limitations.

While a multitude of future experiences are possible, only the most dominant probability is usually foreseen. Interestingly, the actual act of predicting an event can inadvertently affect it – usually by reinforcing or contradicting it. Just as our eyes scan the environment for visual changes, precognition analysis possible future outcomes, zeroing in on the most probable one.

• Clairvoyance is awareness of a current event from afar – i.e., knowing something is happening in the "now" moment. It is often described as similar to viewing a negative of a photograph, where the darks are perceived as light and the whites are perceived with dark overtones. Thus it is like "video x-ray" vision. Clairvoyants also receive their prophetic visions in symbolic form. Their Conscious Minds must then interpret the symbolic presentations so as to decipher their meaning. This is why predictions are sometimes faulty – because the message can be misinterpreted.

• Telepathy is the ability to read another's thoughts, as is commonly understood. Although most of us do not consider ourselves telepathic, occasionally we pick up someone's mental message because it is imbued with a powerful feeling or sense of urgency. At times, the Conscious Mind will happen to be in a receptive state at just the right moment. For example, we have all shared the odd feeling of being stared at; looking around, we find that it was not our imagination. This type of experience validates the existence of some type of unseen energy exchange between humans.

Telepathic messages are sent as symbols and infused with emotional energy. The Subconscious Mind, which likely is the telepathic transporter, operates with symbolic representations. Everything we hear, read, speak or send is instantly relayed to the Subconscious as meaningful symbols. The stronger the emotion, the deeper the experience is engraved within the Subconscious.

• Psychokinesis is different from other psi abilities in that it is pro-active rather than receptive in nature. It is the ability to mentally influence or move material objects – totally by mind power, without any physical contact. In its most simplest form, the ability is displayed via the Ouija board or divining rod (dowsing).

Our Birthright. It is unfortunate that psi abilities are at times considered "kooky" because there is nothing odd about them. Psi abilities are our birthright, and it is only a matter of time before humanity accepts them as natural gifts. Nor are psi abilities superficial experiences but a true reflection of the human equation. Thus we must embrace them as part of who we are, for they already are an inherent expression within us all. Eventually, psi abilities will propel humanity into higher evolutionary gear, for they will help us understand our true role as co-creators with Life.

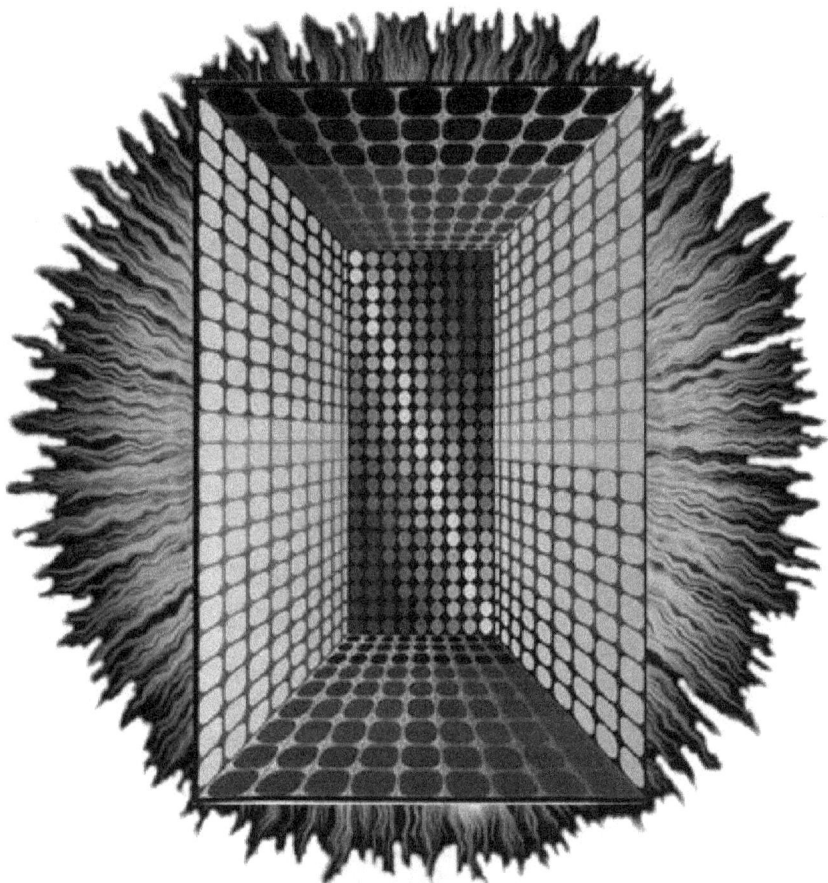

CHAPTER TWO

THE MIND DIMENSION

The human mind is an extremely intricate yet elegant essence. In fact, it is an essence which incorporates the real you! If this revelation serves to awaken and inspire you, then the author's intention will be fulfilled.

We are much more than we can presently comprehend. But if we keep our minds open with this understanding, we can become aware of some of our potential. And we will come to understand that the mind and brain are two separate things, that we are not our bodies but our consciousness.

The ultimate question then may be, "What is consciousness?" Whereas physiologists believe that consciousness is created by the brain, metaphysicians know that consciousness actually comes before the development of the brain. In other words, our consciousness is not simply a byproduct of the inter-workings of chemical components. Our body is not a mannequin in which we are imprisoned. Rather, our creative identity helped create our body so that it can serve as a temple for our consciousness. Coming first, consciousness forms an energy field which directs manifestation of the physical body.

Even more, it is important to understand that we are not our beliefs, actions or thoughts. We are not limited to our expressions, for frequencies are always changeable. We are simply our consciousness — which is our ever eternal essence.

Most of us have not learned to use our consciousness to its fullest extent. We take our mental faculties of imagination, emotion and reason for granted. As a result, our potential capabilities go unused. For example, individuals who are properly trained are able to project their consciousness outside their physical body. This process is known as astral projection (AP). Yet most mainstream individuals find this concept unusual and surreal.

Needless to say, skeptics argue that consciousness projection is simply a hallucinatory experience. To a degree, they are correct, for all of our experiences really take place within the mind: The senses first feed information to the mind, and the mind then creates experiences based on the input. This is the case whether we travel physically or only mentally. According to this theory, no movement actually occurs during astral projection, because dimensional planes are only points on the spectrum of consciousness. When an individual projects his or her astral body, they simply move it from point to point within their consciousness. This is quite similar to tuning a television set to various stations, with the TV remaining stationary at all times.

The mind is indeed much more complex than current scientific theories have offered, for it inhabits a universe of multiple dimensions – domains that are very "real." And experiencing them can be quite fascinating! Individuals who have investigated other realms often note that space and time do not exist within them in the same way they do within our three-dimensional (3D) world.

The Multi-dimensional Mind. Throughout the evolution of the human species, its most valuable asset has been its mind. But we must not confuse the mind with the brain, for they are completely different: The mind uses the brain to express its will; whereas, the mind is our true essence.

Although the mind is really one element, yet it can be divided into three sub types to better understand its characteristics: (1) Conscious, (2) Subconscious and (3) Superconscious. Working in unison, each mind has a distinct set of abilities and purposes. To best understand the complexity of our triad mind, we can use the analogy of an iceberg. Imagine a large iceberg in the ocean – the Conscious and Subconscious minds are akin to the iceberg, but the Superconscious Mind is the endless ocean! And just as the vastness of the ocean implies great depth and energy, such is the tremendous power of the Superconscious. In contrast, the Conscious Mind only constitutes the tip of the iceberg; and the Subconscious Mind is the massive portion of the iceberg beneath the water's surface.

• The Conscious Mind. This mind is neither the most important or least important of the three. But because it tends to be the predominant one within our 3D reality, it is the first one to be described. Although the ego and Conscious Mind are intricately related, it is important to understand that they are not the same thing. While the ego is a projection of willpower, our Conscious Mind is the mechanism it uses to move through reality.

Embedded within the Conscious Mind, the ego is the "filter" through which the Self perceives physical reality. As the container of the ego, the Conscious Mind is specialized to look outward into the physical world, perceiving and assessing the world at all times. It is naturally curious, quite capable of examining reality, whether the data comes from external or internal sources.

Unfortunately, through eons of mis-direction, the Conscious Mind has learned to focus only on physical reality. With this rigid perception, the ego has been able to maintain firm control of our consciousness. This problematic situation manifests in the form of false beliefs. The good news is that we can retrain the Conscious Mind to ask valid questions – to examine all our beliefs in an objective manner. We can learn to discriminate among various beliefs, carefully choosing those which empower us, for our reality is limited according to our beliefs. In fact, our beliefs direct our consciousness; that is, our reality is developed according to our beliefs.

The true value of the ego/Conscious Mind is its ability to make decisions and change direction as needed. As an important projection of the Conscious Mind, the ego promotes our survival in the physical world. In fact, the ego's primary function is to ensure survival.

As the center of our Consciousness Mind, the ego constantly monitors and evaluates the world. It proudly acts as the director of our focus. This is no small feat, since without our egos our bodies would not have survived long enough to experience worldly adventures. You see, as a species our original motivation for physical existence was to explore the third dimensional world. But this objective was mostly sidetracked by the ego's obsession with survival.

Since the ego reasons for us, many psychologists have theorized that this capacity separates us from the other animals. While animals are governed primarily by instinct, humans have the capacity to remember, judge and predict through reasoning. It gives us the power to deduce consequences from premises and to then base our free will on this process.

As higher dimensional entities, most of us can recognize that all humans are equally important. However, the ego invented the idea that one's individuality is more important than all others. Thus habits such as hoarding were developed as a means to ensure individual security. Yet greed is contrary to spiritual understanding – which is to ensure that everyone receive their fundamental physical needs. Unfortunately, the ego has come to feel threatened by spiritual insights. Thus it continually attempts to keep our awareness focused on the material realm. It continues to perceive spirituality as impractical and even boring at times. Relying on reason and judgement alone, the ego rationalizes away intuition and inspiration as impractical assets. Thus we are challenged to ultimately listen to our Higher Selves, to objectively decide whether other modes of thinking are worthy of our endeavors.

On the other hand, the ego is not something to be scorned, for it is an integral part of our humanity. It must be understood for what it is: an expression of our desire to survive in the world. In some ways, it resembles a primitive mind more than a projection of the mind. Nevertheless, it is important to emphasize that it can be trained to work for higher aspirations; it can be taught to refrain from sabotaging our spiritual efforts. We can learn to think outside the conventional box. Even as it continues its efforts at securing our future, the ego can be trained to embrace higher endeavors. For example, it can be trained to appreciate imagination and inspiration, for without hope and revelation there can be no passion for physical survival.

One of the ego's habits is to dichotomize everything into categories of "good" and "bad." It constantly interferes in our decision making by re-enforcing the concept of negative versus positive. In this manner, the ego attempts to block out spiritual insights. It attempts to distract us from the higher things in Life, always placing personal well-being over the good of all humanity. Of course, self-preservation is important, but it must be done with equilibrium within a happy medium. Yet if we remain stuck with polarizations, we are never able to appreciate experiences for their deeper beauty.

To retrain the ego, we must pay close attention to how it works, the manner by which it deceives us into taking dark perspectives. Fortunately, our Superconscious Mind continually works to impress us with higher insights. For example, it incessantly projects the understanding that **we are not on this planet to suffer but to mold reality into a higher frequency** – one based on concepts of unity, joy and creativity.

The emphasis made here is that all three minds work together, as each has a specialty. By means of willpower, the Conscious Mind impresses patterns upon the Subconscious Mind. As long as our Conscious Mind remains in positive mode it gives constructive commands to the Submind. Since the lower mind is unable to rationalize, it simply submits to mental patterns that are impressed upon it. The stronger the feeling, the more resonant the imprint upon the Submind. Thus it is extremely important that we take great care in planting self-empowering patterns. Otherwise, it is quite possible to literally harvest nightmares.

• The Subconscious Mind. While our ego uses the Conscious Mind to command our lives, the Subconscious records our thought patterns. Like the iceberg portion floating beneath the surface of water, the Submind has a vast, yet hidden potential. And this potential can manifest in unlimited expressions.

The Submind may appear mysterious and uncontrollable. Yet, the opposite is true: considering all the automatic activities it runs in our bodies – metabolism, circulation and breathing, e.g. – it should be clear that its main purpose is to function as a computer. And being computer-like, the Submind works much like the auto-pilot of an aircraft. It is extremely impressionable, mirroring strong thoughts which originate in the Conscious Mind. Its programming is also similar to that of computer software, storing personality traits and beliefs that are impressed upon it through the years. These traits include habits, attitudes, prejudices, philosophies and memories. In fact, it remembers everything, and holds images of self-worth, whether they be good or bad.

Since the Submind is unable to make conclusions or rationalizations; these are left to the Conscious Mind. It merely accepts the impressions from conscious reasoning, moving them into deliberate action, just as a computer operates according to input by human beings. In other words, it is not a function of the Submind to examine beliefs but to follow and implement them. Thus our thoughts and beliefs are its directives. Knowing this, we should consciously impress thoughts of hope and confidence, rather than thoughts of doubt and negativity. It is important to remember that the Submind records and stores everything we experience – what we believe, hear, see and feel. And it doesn't matter whether these experiences are real or imagined, for it takes all perceptions in a literal fashion.

When we act habitually, direction comes from the Subconscious Mind. Once we learn how these two minds work together, we can apply the working principles to establish new productive habits. Once constructive habits are firmly established, we can then focus our consciousness on other important matters. Of course, the benefits of mental implants are only as powerful as the ego allows! Thus it is important to establish the habit of self-analysis, which enables us to rise above erroneous beliefs.

We should always remember that the ego can be a trickster of logic, often rejecting new ideas because they appear contrary to established critical thought. The "Law of Inertia" also operates in the mental arena, meaning that old habits will tend to remain ingrained. If we are too lazy, it will be difficult to overcome their power. It is, however, possible to gradually modify them. We don't have to change overnight! As we gradually erode resistance to new ideas, we can simultaneously nurture new ones – as in the classic affirmation: "Everyday, in every way, I am getting better and better!"

When new habits are first initiated, we are painfully conscious of every effort towards establishing them. But as we persevere, our Subconscious Mind increasingly takes over more of the effort. Gradually, the Submind is able to lessen the need for conscious effort. Since our views become increasingly fixed as we get older, it is important to understand the process of establishing new habits. As we age, our willingness to accept new facts usually continues to narrow in perspective. This is a problematic situation, because then only shocking effects can break the way for new ideas. Stubborn personalities especially need constant re-programming, but they are usually too inhibited, fearful, anxious and repressed to grow. Other than shock treatment, the solution is to nurture flexibility as a foundational habit, teaching the ego the importance of innovation.

Subliminal suggestions are a powerful means of reprogramming the Subconscious. Audio and video programs are manifestations of this technique. Whether we decide to stop smoking, improve our business skills or boost our confidence, we can implant new patterns by means of powerful affirmations. In fact, we can adjust any area of our lives in which we have direct control — such as improving our determination, attitude and health. Even changes in cell nutrition can be modified through suggestion, because the metabolic process is controlled by the Subconscious Mind.

Even without technology, our ancestors knew how to apply suggestion via trancing. They may not have shared the same terminology, but they were nevertheless quite capable of modifying their mental programming through traditional ritual or meditation. Meditation is an ancient means of affirming positive suggestions. When specific thought patterns are habitually re-enforced through any type of meditation, they eventually gain momentum of their own. This is because patterns are the most powerful gateway into the mind.

•The Superconscious Mind. While the Subconscious is the receptacle of habits, and the Conscious is the director of our focus, the Supermind is our connection to the vast primordial essence. It is our connection to Life and has infinite resources at its command. Its essence can be likened to an ocean of pure energy, having the same quality as a Universal Mind. The difference between the Superconscious and the Universal Mind is really only one of degree. Through the ages, many mystics have learned to consciously access their Superconscious Mind, thus empowering themselves with miraculous experiences.

In fact, we are ultimately projections of the Superconscious Mind into 3D reality. In other words, it has given us our existence. Eventually, via the Supermind, we will come to understand much more than our Conscious Mind can only begin to grasp. The Supermind is the conduit through which the universe speaks to us and by which all humanity is connected with the Higher Source. Intuition, insight, inspiration — these are all communications from the sea of Life.

When we listen to our inner voice, we gain valuable guidance. This inner voice, also known as intuition, originates with our Superconscious Mind — our Higher Self. Because it originates in a timeless, spaceless dimension, our Supermind is able to transcend both time and space, giving us access to a vista where the past and future merge. Our Conscious Mind can learn to transcend linear time with assistance from the Supermind. It can learn to unfocus from the five basic senses, allowing it to perceive via psi senses. One way to train for intuitive reception is through meditation. As the normal senses are quieted— silencing both logic and imagination — a direct connection can be made with the Higher Self.

The Collective Unconscious is another type of mind. Every human grouping — from workshops to family gatherings – develops a collective field of consciousness. Whenever conscious energies are shared, they collect and coalesce into one comprehensive field. By this principle, humanity has developed a Collective Unconscious mind in which are stored its unique energy patterns. It is a storehouse of memory for all of humanity's endeavors. Not only does each individual contribute to the Collective Unconscious but so does the human species as a whole.

In fact, it is theorized that because the brain does not contain enough space to store all memories, it functions mostly as a retrieval mechanism. Accordingly, the brain functions somewhat like a television receiver, retrieving and transmitting data via electromagnetic frequencies. Thus the Conscious Mind relies on information retrieved from the Collective as well as Superconscious Mind on a day to day basis.

As the source of intuitive and inspirational thought, our Superconscious Mind constantly attempts to inspire us with a clear view of reality. Unfortunately, the ego has mostly embraced erroneous ideas which tend to block out higher insights, preferring to focus on physical reality. For too long, the ego has misled humanity into believing that there is no other reality other than the third dimensional one.

Yet the ultimate reality is that we inhabit a universe of multiple dimensions with very tangible realities. These other dimensions are not simply products of imagination; rather, they have a coherence of their own. One difference is that, whereas our 3D world is a joint creation by humanity, some of the other dimensions exist as individual realities — meaning that individuals are free to create their personal worlds.

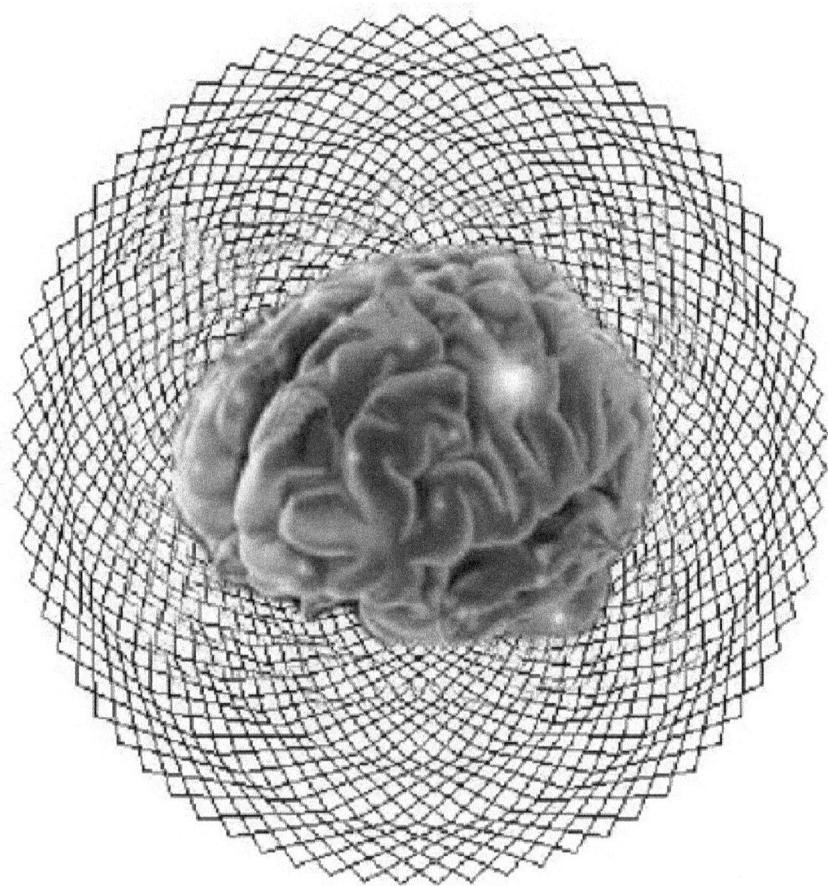

CHAPTER THREE

THE TRANSCEIVER BRAIN

Those who wish to realize their full potential know that the mind and brain are two distinct essences. While the mind is our true nature, the brain is the means by which we express our frequencies upon the world. In fact, the brain's most important function is that of a transmitter and receiver of frequency – a transceiver of energy patterns. Research has indicated that we receive some of our ideas via energy transmissions, which are very much like radio signals. These energy transmissions exist all around us, extending throughout all reality.

There is an medium known as the Universal Matrix, which holds and transmits all ideas. The

Matrix is known by other names as well: the Universal Lattice, Quantum Canvas, Hyperspace and the Akash. This medium is an endless labyrinth within which the superstrings of the universe vibrate rhythmically, as they beat the Laws of Creation. Thus the connection between the Matrix and matter is analogous to that of musical strings. The constant force of consciousness sets the frequencies and varies them according to the dimensional locale. In fact, the Universal Matrix is both a mirror and a container for everything that manifests in Life. Its purpose is to reflect energy perfectly — especially that of thought energy.

Based on the premise of the Universal Matrix, one can understand that the brain functions as a transceiver of reality – being able to both broadcast and receive thought patterns from the universal canvas. Thus the brain accesses information from the Matrix as needed, functioning more like a quantum computer as it organizes information holographically and stores only the most basic facts.

Furthermore, it is via the Superconscious Mind that our brains derive many of our creative thoughts in a form known as intuition.

The Dualistic Brain. That the mind and brain are two separate properties is supported by several facts — including the fact that there are individuals with no detectable brain and yet able to function relatively well in society. IQ tests given to these individuals have proven them to be of average intelligence. Obviously, the existence of these individuals indicates that the human mind is able to function even without a complete brain. Considering the amount of information that the brain processes on a daily basis, it appears that it cannot possibly hold all the knowledge with which it is credited. Indications are that the brain serves mostly as an information retrieval mechanism.

The dualistic nature of the brain has also helped develop human consciousness as it now exists. Besides aiding development of curiosity, its duality probably enabled the development of higher self awareness. Furthermore, due to its two hemispheres, our brain developed two types of consciousness:

• one which is rational, linear and cognitive;

• the other which is holistic, intuitive and artistic.

In other words, each brain hemisphere has a unique way of perceiving reality; but together they have promoted our unparalleled way of thinking. The distinction is between objective versus intuitive thinking, or impartial analysis versus subjective insight.

The Left Hemisphere. The left side of the brain controls the right side of the body. It tends to handle thought patterns dealing with linear, quantitative processes – such as mathematics, measurement of time, logic, deduction, rationalization and analytical thought. It is more dominant with calculations, math and logical abilities. Generally speaking, it prefers parts (rather than the whole), function, symbols, instruction and structure.

The Right Hemisphere. The right side of the brain controls the left side of the body. It is focused on comprehensive, qualitative thinking, which includes creativity, pattern recognition, symmetry, comparisons, imagination, artistic appreciation, healing, intuition and abstract thought. It is more dominant with spatial abilities, face recognition, visual imagery and music. Generally speaking, the right brain prefers the whole (rather than parts), appearances, pictures and spontaneity.

Needless to say, the ideal is to encourage a balance between our left and right brain thinking, for the combination of logic and intuition leads to our fullest potential. Many other aspects of the brain are worthy of understanding, but covering them is beyond this book's objective. However, there is one gland worthy of mention – the pineal. This mysterious gland will be discussed in the next chapter.

Behavior & the Brain. Although the brain's predominant function is that of a transceiver, it also affects our behavior. There is no denying the importance of bio-psychology, which is the measuring of biological variables in an attempt to relate them to specific behavior. The theory of a quantum layer to the brain does not undermine psychology in any form or fashion.

Most likely, there are at least three behavioral patterns that are influenced by the brain's chemistry: altruism, sexual orientation and extra sensory perception (ESP):

• Altruism. Because performing good acts without reward does not seem to provide an edge for the individual, it has been a mystery as to why they are exercised at all. The answer may be that people are wired to be in tune with the needs of others. Not only is the brain wired to communicate with the Universal Matrix, but it is also programmed to give the individual a social conscience. The region of the brain known as the Posterior Superior Temporal Cortex (pSTC) promotes altruistic acts as needed. This activity has been observed using the MRI (Magnetic Resonance Imaging). However, wiring in the pSTC is not focused on a reward system but on perceiving the intentions of others. It seems to be associated with meaningful stimuli. It is not clear why pSTC activity gets ramped up during altruistic acts, for there is no real cause-and-effect relationship between the two. But there is a definite biological relationship between altruism and brain activity.

• Sexual Orientation. The issue of an individual's attraction to either gender is also based on specific brain development. Research findings increasingly indicate that sexual orientation is based on brain structuring. Using MRI technology, the brains of straight men and women have been contrasted to those of gay men and women. In comparing brain symmetry, it became apparent that the brains of gay men tend to be similar in structure to those of straight women. And gay women's brains tend to be like those of straight men – where the right hemisphere tends to be slightly larger than the left one.

One other difference is that the hypothalamus is larger in straight men and gay women. Certainly, researchers have speculated whether brain differences are the result of experience rather than genetics causing the difference. However, differing brain structures are more likely reflections of genetic factors, because they seem to predetermine a person's sexual orientation. In other words, most individuals know their orientation even before their brains develop to maturity. Thus a biological basis for gender orientation will be reinforced with future findings.

• Extra-Sensory Perception. Because each individual is really a mental entity, the insight helps us understand why ESP is able to work. For example, when we follow our intuition we are receiving incoming thought frequencies. And although no specific mechanism for telepathy has been found, it has been established that each brain lobe resonates with different electromagnetic frequencies. These EM waves have been recorded with an EEG (electroencephalograph), and they have consistently registered slightly different on each lobe. Due to its dualistic nature, a type of resonance develops between the two lobes, theoretically establishing telepathic waves.

A range of brain frequencies has been categorized as follows:

NAME	FREQUENCY	STATE
DELTA	0.5Hz - 3.0Hz	deep sleep
THETA	4.0Hz - 7.0Hz	drowsiness
ALPHA	8.0Hz - 12Hz	relaxed but alert
BETA	13Hz - 30Hz	highly alert

GAMMA	40Hz	highest perception

As we can see, each frequency predisposes us to specific states of mind. The theta frequency range is the one which is most conducive to various types of ESP. At this range, ego boundaries tend to dissolve and are replaced with a wider sense of consciousness.

For thousands of years, humans have been using brainwave tuners to alter the mind into a trance state. Various methods have been used. Cavemen undoubtedly used psychoactive plants to induce deep trancing, probably while watching a fire at night. Under the right circumstances, a campfire alone can induce an altered state, as flickering of the lights can be hypnotic. Then monks practiced brainwave entrainment by means of meditation. Now, in modern times, science researchers have learned how to induce trance by means of binaural frequencies. This technology is known as Hemisphere Synchronization (or Hemisync), which can impact a whole range of mental states. When brain frequencies are modified – whether by means of chemistry, meditation or technology – we can modify a subject's mental state. By matching a specific brain frequency, researchers can literally make an individual receptive to telepathy. With the right technology, a subject's brain can even be made to resonate like that of a great mystic – simply with a flick of a switch!

Hemisync is based on the concept of "binaural beats" – i.e., sound resonance between the left and right hemispheres. During a Hemisync procedure, the mind automatically tunes in to the frequency that the two tones generate jointly. By inputting different tones in each ear, the result is a third frequency known as the "beat frequency." In reality, this joint frequency is heard only by the brain and not the ears.

The Power of Suggestibility. When we think

about our drives and responses, we should think of the brain as a container for our Conscious, Subconscious and Superconscious minds. Subliminal affirmations (also known as auto-suggestion or programmed rehearsal) can be powerful tools for developing the mind. Think of them as software programming for the mind. Affirmations can help us re-enforce objectives – such as building confidence, releasing fears, expressing creativity, improving performance and much more. But they must be used consistently for the process to have lasting impact. Of course, affirmations can never replace medicine, although they can re-enforce many medical practices.

Subliminal affirmation may seem mysterious but only because there is so much we do not understand about the mind. Two principles that can work during auto-programming of the mind are:
• Suggestibility - when subjects are able to suspend critical thinking suggestions can program the mind with new objectives; and

• Hyperaesthesia - the senses can be heightened in this state of mind: hearing, vision, smell, touch, memory and even ESP can be enhanced.

Knowing of these two principles helps strip some of the mystery around the principle of affirmation because it helps us objectify how the mind works. The more we understand the principles that function within the mind, the better we are able to develop "psychological equations" for enhancing the mind.

Susceptibility to suggestion is common to all humans of average intelligence. Closely related to suggestibility is hypnotic suggestion, which can serve as a direct means to reprogramming the mind. Ailments with mental origins – such as emotional conflicts — can be more easily resolved when approached with this tool. Although some subjects can be simply "talked" into alleviating their ailment, implanting hypnotic suggestions is a much more powerful process which leads to stronger, faster and deeper results. Because thoughts "color" our psychological and physiological structures, any part of the body can be affected by hypnotic suggestions — although physiological origins must addressed simultaneously. In this spirit, the American Medical Association has embraced the power of hypnotic suggestion as a valid medical tool. In fact, affirmation, auto-suggestion and hypnotic suggestion are all based on the same principles, differences simply being one of degree.

It is important to realize that a hypnotist is never fully in control of the hypnotic session, that hypnosis is really a process of self-hypnosis. That is, hypnosis works only because the subject willingly transfers his or her conscious control to the hypnotist. This is true, even if the subject is not fully conscious of the process. Thus hypnosis implies acceptance and enactment of suggestions, which is a feat only possible with a high degree of consciousness. When a subject associates hypnosis with an aura of mystery, this renders him or her even more susceptible to its powers of persuasion. On the other hand, becoming informed on the mechanics of hypnotic suggestion does not diminish its powers – it can actually help a subject become a more effective partner in the process.

Ultimately, the power of suggestion is based on logic. It is logical succession that increases a subject's conformance to more suggestion. Once a belief is established, other suggestions can be added in logical sequence. When based on "truths" that the subject accepts as real, it is easier to logically move to other related facts. Thus the subject assists with the "force feeding" of beliefs. Of course, the instrumentality of suggestion is in itself neither good nor bad. As with any tool, it depends on how it is used.

Mass Suggestibility. It may be surprising that national character is also susceptible to mass suggestion. Modern anthropologists will attest that cultural climate is due more to national suggestion than to heredity. The United States of America is an excellent example of how individuals from different racial and cultural backgrounds become American in action as well as outlook. This often develops in only one generation. As a new generation grows up, it finds national suggestions played out all around them. By this means, they absorb "American" mannerisms, beliefs and practices – much the way a sponge absorbs liquids.

Social psychologists are aware that crowds can also instill mass suggestion within individuals. Unfortunately, the collective psyche of a crowd is usually of the lowest common denominator – i.e., it is inferior to the average individual minds comprising it. Thus mass suggestion can lead to dangerous mob scenes.

Mass sentiment can be manipulated by various means:
• literature and advertisements,
• organizations and government,

• art and sports.

Most of us absorb suggestions channeled through these avenues because we do not have the time or ability to test all propositions. Therefore, we accept them as valid, based simply on faith. Otherwise, we would be incapable of assimilating societal "truths."

Principles of Hypno-Suggestion. While suggestion can be a matter of applying the right beliefs and expectations during a hypnotic session, there is one other factor that deepens suggestibility – attention. Thus the best equation for planting suggestions is "belief + expectation + attention = suggestibility":

• Belief. The subject must have faith in the competence, integrity and logic of the suggestion.

• Expectation. The subject must accept the logical sequence of expectations. When the hypnotic equation is followed correctly, both belief and expectation become intertwined, amplifying suggestibility, impulsiveness and imagination.

• Attention. When the Conscious Mind is distracted,

it is kept from blocking out suggestions, making it easier to infiltrate the Subconscious Mind with ideas. Among other things, a distraction can consist of a voice, music or hypnotic object.

Acuity of reason is the biggest hindrance to suggestibility, because it is the ego analyzing and objecting to new ideas. When the ego (within the Conscious Mind) is perfectly relaxed or distracted, its allows for implantation of suggestions in the Submind. Furthermore, when a subject sustains enough belief in a concept, the belief enhances its probable success. There is, however, a difference between "wishing" and "expecting" – and expectation will always win over simple wishing. Thus results are most likely when belief, expectation and attention are integrated within an equation.

One of the best tools for auto-suggestion is music, because it preoccupies the Conscious Mind while simultaneously affecting the emotional center. Thus music can reach the Subconscious quite effectively. Speech, on the other hand, is often ignored. Whatever the objective may be, music can help shape emotions towards a specific objective.

Tool of the Past & Future. Needless to say, much more will be understood in the future regarding the employment of suggestibility. But it already has a very long history of usage by humanity. In the earliest days, it was applied in religious rites. From Egyptian ceremonies, to Greek temples, and then to re-invention in the 18th century as mesmerism, hypno-suggestion eventually blossomed into a modern science in its own right. Although some critics will claim that auto-suggestion and hypnosis are based on mere imagination, these same critics cannot deny that imagination is a powerful state in itself. Indeed, hypno-suggestion is a powerful means for directing the imagination towards specific goals.

In a nutshell, auto-suggestion is about

deciding what we want, implanting those ideas firmly in our minds – then nurturing them into full expression. Because imagination is a power in its own right, it has predominance over willpower. For example, if we desire something, it is only after expressing the desire that we focus our willpower on the objective. Imagery actually moves our willpower into motion. Where imagination and desire lead, willpower follows. Thus, like seeds that are properly planted and nurtured, ideas eventually sprout from our imagination into the 3D world.

Even though the power of suggestion is often used to control us – even to demoralize us at times – we can apply its power for self-enhancement. We can rise above any sense of worthlessness, feelings of inadequacy or despair – and reach the pinnacle of our potential. The same tool that has been used to manipulate us can be turned to our advantage. Furthermore, we can learn to amplify the transmitter aspect of our minds; we can create by projecting specific frequencies. We do not have to simply receive orders from the powers that be. In other words, we can become actors rather than simply re-actors to circumstances.

86

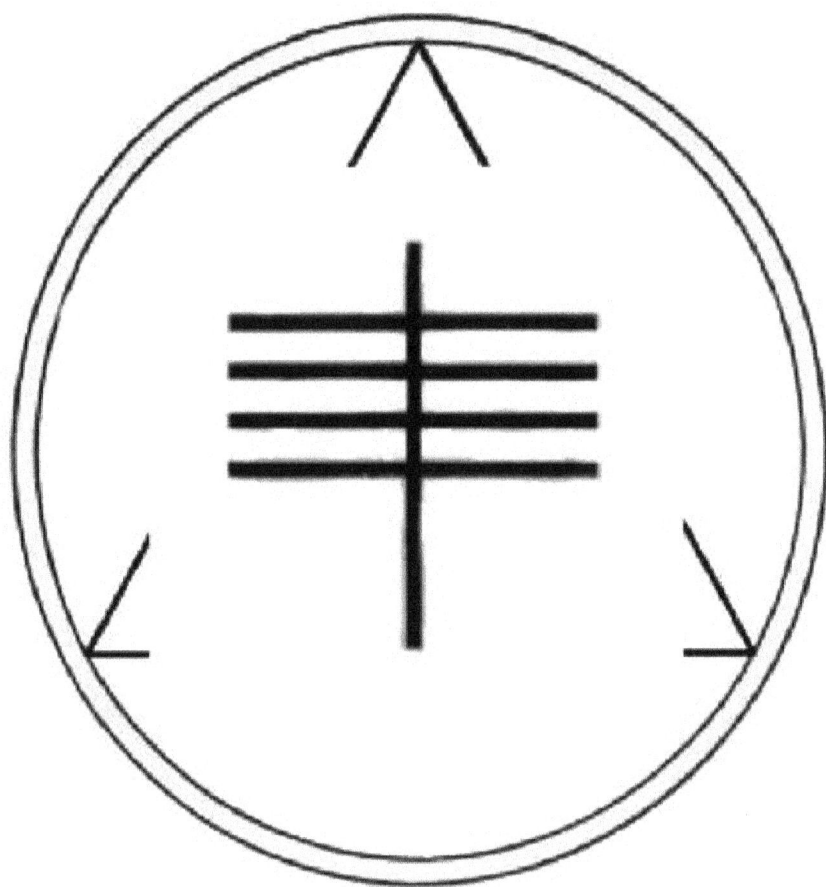

CHAPTER FOUR

PINEAL - LIGHTNING ROD

Of all the glands, the pineal is perhaps the most mysterious. Ever since the human body was first investigated, researchers have been struggling to understand the pineal's full functions and yet have been unable to do so. Very little documentation exists on its role, but it certainly has a rich metaphysical reputation. For one thing, philosophers and metaphysicians have considered it the "seat of the soul." From time immemorial, the pineal gland has been known as the Third Eye – the divine eye for spiritual vision. If it is indeed a third eye, then it may prove to be of paramount importance to the development of humanity.

For over 2000 years, the pineal has remained

an anatomical curiosity. For one thing, its appearance is so insignificant that researchers first considered it as useless as the appendix. Both were considered residual, vestigial organs, throwbacks to earlier reptilian animals. However, that attitude has been gradually changing as new discoveries have spotlighted the pineal's central importance in the production of several hormones and enzymes. Although all probable functions of the pineal gland are still a mystery, it is becoming clear that it is not obsolete nor useless.

In the distant past, the pineal may have been at least ten times larger than it is today, having shrunk to the size of a pea in modern humans. However it is becoming evident that the gland is unique in each individual, showing extreme variability in size, form and internal structure. Although relatively large in children, it tends to shrink and calcify during adulthood. It continues to harden and atrophy as we age, but there are exceptions. Some individuals are allegedly able to exercise it and keep it vital.

In terms of physical description, it lacks glamour and size. Attached to the base of the brain, it is reddish-gray in color and conical in shape – vaguely resembling a tiny pine cone, which is the reason for its name. It is unique in that it holds a solitary status within the brain, whereas other brain sites tend to be paired with a counterpart.

Although surrounded by the brain, the pineal is not derived from brain tissue. Rather, it develops from specialized tissue from the roof of the mouth; it then eventually migrates to the center of the brain. Autopsies have also revealed that the pineal and pituitary glands sometimes fuse together in some individuals.

Besides hardening by the age of twelve, the pineal gland also gradually decreases production of neuro-transmitters. This is around the age that people stop dreaming of flying, and their ability to see mystical things often ceases as well. Interestingly, it has been discovered during autopsies that the pineal gland is underdeveloped in the mentally retarded. Furthermore, it appears that there is a connection between gland size and psi ability: the larger the pineal, the more likely the individual exhibits ESP.

Rhythmic Function. Although the highest function of the pineal may not be completely known for some time, some of its hormonal effects are now well established. Its most fundamental function apparently is to regulate the body's internal clock: directing sexual maturation, sleep patterns, as well as other circadian cycles. It is considered a master gland because it is responsible for the regulation of various other endocrine glands as well. For example, by secreting the hormone melatonin and working closely with the hypothalamus, the pineal is able to direct the body's biorhythms – such as those related to thirst, hunger, sexual desire, aging and sleep. The gland also possesses the highest level of serotonin anywhere in the body. Serotonin is a crucial precursor for tryptamine, a critical step for other important secretions. Furthermore, unique enzymes that convert serotonin into natural psychedelic compounds are present in extra-ordinarily high concentrations in the pineal.

In some animals, the pineal gland serves more than to simply regulate bio-rhythms; it appears to function as a center for navigation as well. Apparently the gland contains extremely minute amounts of magnetic material, known as magnetosomes, allowing it to monitor magnetic fields and thereby aligning the body to it. This appears to be the case, because changing the surrounding magnetic fields alters the animals' ability to orient themselves. Thus it appears that the gland can serve to receive and transmit electromagnetic waves.

Lightning Rod. Having the second highest

blood flow after the kidneys, it appears that pineal secretions are of utmost importance. In fact, this concentrated bundle of nerves may serve as something more than a chemical factory – it may be a transceiver of subtle electromagnetism. While not actually a part of the brain, the pineal has a strategic closeness to the emotional centers of the brain and spinal cord. This prime location gives it potential as an electro-magnetic lightning rod for different states of mind. Sounds, electro-magnetic waves and hormonal secretions appear to activate it, thus causing it to vibrate as an antenna and gateway into multiple dimensional states.

Location is certainly very important, and the fact that the pineal lies well-protected in a central location, deep inside the brain, may underline its importance. Thus it serves as a central connection for several processes. Several factors indicate its importance: First, it is surrounded by cerebrospinal fluid. Second, it is strategically close to the emotional and sensory brain locales. Third, it is connected to the thalamus, hypothalamus, basil nuclei and medial temporal lobe. Lastly, from its unique perch, this gland nearly touches visual and auditory sensory relays. Thus the pineal has direct access to much of the brain's assets, and its position allows for instant, direct delivery of its unique chemical secretions into the cerebrospinal fluid.

The Legendary Third Eye. Its central location in the brain, as well as its presence in other species, indicates that the pineal gland is an older part of humanity's evolutionary brain system. Interestingly, studies have found that the pineal contains light-sensitive cells which function like those of the eye's retina, testifying to the fact that the pineal gland can "see." In fact, in some lower vertebrates it actually manifests as an eye-like structure; in others, though not organized as an eye, it functions as a light receptor. When it manifests as an eye in some species, it possesses a lens, cornea and retina like an ordinary eye – although in reverse format! Thus third eyes appear to be mirror images of regular eyes and unable to serve for regular vision.

Although nerves connect the eyes directly with the pineal, the connection detours through the neck before reaching the gland. Yet, due to its strategic location, it is still able to affect the visual and auditory brain centers. Theoretically, the pineal gland may have developed in humans to serve as a vehicle for psychic "vision." Although this theory is controversial, it has not been disproven nor has the idea been shaken by any evidence to the contrary.

Of course, skeptics scoff at the possibility of a third eye, but they need only research and they will find that it actually exists in various species throughout the planet. The idea of a physical third eye is not incredible – it is a fact! The animals that do possess a third eye do so with a complete functional lens. Usually, the eye is found below transparent skin, allowing light to reach and activate it. From fish to lizards to mice the level of pineal development varies. Nevertheless, the fact that Nature has developed physical eyes out of the pineal gland should make critics think twice about dismissing the concept.

The best living proof of a third eye may be the Tuatara reptile of New Zealand, in which it is quite prominent on the back of its head. Although covered with translucent skin, it has all the essential features of a regular eye: because it contains cells similar to the retina of a regular eye, it may have full capacity for vision. Just like a regular eye, it possesses a lens, cornea and retina.

Multi-Dimensional Vision. Although there is little information on the full potential of the pineal gland, mythology states that long ago all humans were able to naturally see multi-dimensionally. Allegedly, all humans possessed active, fully formed pineal glands which allowed them to view the finer dimensions in Life.

As a receiver and transmitter (transceiver) of electro-magnetic frequency, it is no coincidence that the pineal has been associated with a third eye. Individuals who personally experience its awesome power describe it is as a natural telescope and microscope wrapped in one. A fully developed pineal allows an individual to reach his or her full creative potential, for it is a priceless jewel, a key which unlocks and reveals the magical side of Life!

Whereas normal eyes look outward, the third eye "sees" interdimensionally, outward and inward. The higher evolved a species, the deeper the pineal has moved into the brain. For example, while the bird pineal no longer sits on top of its skull, it remains sensitive to external light via a paper-thin bone structure. Mammalian pineals, on the other hand, are not touched directly by light, because they are found deep in the center of the brain. The reason for this may be due to its elevated role as a receptor for finer forms of energy – rather than for perceiving regular light.

As a crystalline structure, the pineal functions on various dimensional levels. That is, it is pro-active not only in the physical realm but also in the astral, etheric and other levels. As an eye for viewing the finer dimensions of Life, it works via the principle of sympathetic resonance. It is a relay point for subtle energies, through which they are processed on their way to and from the body. The process is similar to the way radio waves strike a quartz crystal in a radio transceiver. The crystal resonates with each frequency in such a way as to absorb it, and then it passes it along as audio frequencies. Similarly, the pineal is a crystalline structure that receives information from the finer dimensions, and then it transmits the data to various points of the brain for translation – which often results in intuition, inspiration or dreams. Thus by focusing on the pineal gland, mystics have enhanced their psychic insight.

A developed "psychic eye" is meant to guide us innately through the various energy frequencies in the world. It would give us the ability to rely on objective truth, rather than on mere appearances – for "seeing is believing." Without it, we are often left to trust in blind faith, unable to view the true energetic causes of certain experiences. On the other hand, a fully developed pineal gland allows us to see things of finer quality. Indeed, the wonders of the psychic world lie open to the gaze of those with developed third eyes. All things, including human individuals, are perceived as they really are – beyond their shadowy illusion.

It is impossible to lie to individuals with fully developed pineal glands, for the truth is always clear to them in the form of perceptible energy forms. With third eye vision, it can be determined whether someone is speaking the truth by the way their colors fluctuate. Different colors within a person's aura mean different things. For example, flecks of red can mean pulses of anger. Genuine liking, jealousy and indifference can also be defined by various colors. Individuals who live clean lives are seen to have golden auras. While yellow or gold indicate enlightenment, discolorations can indicate an inability to reason – taking words literally.

Furthermore, a person's health status can be interpreted by the color and intensity of their body energy (aura). Illnesses can be determined by threads of color above an area of the body, indicating that an organ, gland or other body part is out of balance. Of course, always having to see the failings of others can be overwhelming and disconcerting. So seers with third eye vision also learn to shut it off at will.

Doorway to the Superconscious. Another more esoteric purpose of the pineal gland is that of linking the Conscious and Superconscious Minds. In fact, this connection is the biological basis for spiritual experience, because it is the central hub for mental factors that lead to enhanced psi abilities. All senses must have their physical correspondence in the body, and psi senses are based on the pineal, for it transceives psychic phenomena from various dimensional planes. One might say that this gland is the "control center" for subtle energy – a lightning rod for the soul. For this reason, it is also referred to as the "spirit gland," since it supports a variety of altered states of consciousness.

The pineal gland is the link which connects humanity with the auric world. It is the organ through which we are able to perceive and interact with the psychic realm. When it is fully activated, there is the potential for making rapid leaps in spiritual development, as it has the capacity to illuminate angles and shades that are usually unseen to us. In fact, it has been claimed by metaphysicians that, if all records were destroyed, it would still be possible to recover them via our third eye. For allegedly, any and all information can be retrieved from what is known as the Akash Field – a dimension where all information is stored.

Opening the Third Eye. Many factors can

activate the pineal gland – some accidental, some deliberate. Head injuries, eye surgery and drugs have been known to stimulate the pineal into active status. Once activated, it becomes a lightning rod for spiritual communication. Just as the physical body is known to react to electromagnetic frequencies, the pineal is especially sensitive to very fine energy radiations.

The major factors that can stimulate the pineal into fully active status are surgery, meditation, resonance and environment:

• **Surgical Procedure.** The idea of a "third eye" was accepted as fact in some ancient cultures. While there have always been naturally clairvoyant individuals, some cultures practiced physical opening of the third eye. That is, they went beyond simply believing in the third eye and actually opening a hole in the cranium to allow it to function fully. Because it is an extremely difficult procedure, it was performed only by the most skilled doctors.

Ancient Hindu literature refers to this medical procedure:

1) A herbal compress was placed on the forehead, bound tightly in place. After several hours, the compress was removed and the forehead was wiped clean.

2) An instrument having a round shaft in the shape of a "U" and tiny teeth was used to drill a very small hole in the forehead – lending direct access to the gland.

3) With access to the pineal, a sliver of wood was then inserted into the opening using tremendous caution. It was slid inward until a stinging sensation was felt in the bridge of the nose and a blinding flash was seen by the conscious subject.

4) As the metal instrument was carefully removed, the sliver of wood was left and bound in place, remaining there for two or three weeks. Until the sliver was removed, the subject was secluded in a dark room so that proper healing could take place. Immediately after this, the

subject allegedly acquired an enhanced, visual perception of energy, color and subtle scents.

• **Meditation.** This is a less intrusive method for opening the third eye. Although the results are not as instantaneous, the body's bio-energy can be gradually directed into the pineal vortex. When full activation is successful by this means, a sensation of light is experienced, followed by an expansion of consciousness. This process is less likely to cause psychic disequilibrium, because meditation prods the third eye open in a slower, balanced fashion. The right kind of meditation can elicit waves of resonance that affect the chemical properties of the pineal. Furthermore, specific sounds – i.e. mantrums – can intensify this resonance..

• **Resonance.** Technology can be a means for re-awakening the third eye. By physically applying the right resonance in the form of electricity, magnetism or sound, one can achieve amazing mind-altering effects. On the other hand, coarse EM frequencies can suppress pineal activity. Therefore, only magnetic frequencies of a specific pattern are beneficial.

For example, the correct wavelength of light influences production of melatonin in the pineal; it can also affect sexual development. It is known that animals kept in red light show increased gonadal development; while those kept in green light do not. Thus the impact of resonance on the pineal is more than mere speculation.

• **Environment.** Perhaps the smoothest route for activating the third eye is living in a high frequency environment. The implication is that an escalation in the Earth's frequency can awaken third vision in the human race. As various individuals evolve, their personal development can promote psychic capabilities in others within proximity. It is a synergistic dynamism. Not only is humanity gradually awakening, but psychic individuals enhance the process within others simply by living within proximity to others..

The Spirit Molecule. Interestingly, research has found that various hallucinogens concentrate mostly in the pineal and pituitary glands. This may indicate that the neuro receptors here accomodate neuro-transmitters which function similarly to psychedelic drugs. It is also known that mescaline (a natural psychedelic alkaloid) can raise serotonin levels, which is a mood regulator. Furthermore, there is a synergistic relationship between serotonin and melatonin (the main pineal hormone): while serotonin has its highest concentration during the day, melatonin is highest during the night.

The pineal contains high levels of enzymes which transform serotonin into a number of neuro chemicals. One of these is DMT – a very important chemical regarding psi abilities. DMT (dimethyl-tryptamine) has the potent effect of triggering trance-like conditions, including lucid dreaming. In fact, natural hallucinogens may be the reason why children cannot distinguish between fantasy and reality. With the highest concentrations occurring during infancy, these neuro-transmitters tend to decrease after the age of eight.

At this point in time, the strongest hypothesis is that DMT serves as a potent psi chemical. In fact, it may be the key to "alternate realities" – a chemical portal through which our consciousness enters other dimensions. The hypothesis is based on the understanding that DMT can:
• have psychedelic effects;
• occur naturally in the brain and body;
• be sought out by the brain.
Although DMT concentrates especially in the pineal, it is found naturally throughout the body. The hypothesis proposes that excessive DMT production is involved in natural psychedelic states. For example, large amounts occur during near-death and mystical experiences. Interestingly, it also appears to play a role in "alien abduction" experiences – not in a delusional manner but by

actually projecting consciousness into other dimensions.

The DMT hypothesis allows researchers to tie up several loose ends. Although the pineal gland produces several neuro-transmitters, only DMT appears to support the hypothesis adequately. For it is known that DMT opens the senses to profound multi-dimensional experiences.

The pineal's placement is perfect for its function as a lightning rod to psi experiences. Its central location allows its chemicals to easily affect nearby brain centers (such as the pituitary gland). The pineal's neuro chemicals need immediate access to cerebrospinal fluid, and this is why its proximity is essential. For example, if DMT were to first enter the blood stream, enzymes would destroy it long before it could exert mental effects. But because it enters directly into the spinal fluid, simple diffusion is all it takes for sensory and emotional effects. Even a pumping heart is unnecessary for diffusion to take place.

Thus diffusion easily allows for near-death experiences – perhaps even assisting the soul to exit the body. The fact that the pineal is the last active organ in the body at the time of death adds credence to this proposition. As we die, our consciousness shifts into a focused state – most likely via the pineal gland. To make this happen, all the pineal chemicals work together for one final burst, producing what is known as the NDE (near-death experience). These neural factors also combine during the experiences of meditation, birthing and extreme physical stress.

The pineal gland has a purpose much grander than anyone in modern times has been able to fathom. As humanity continues to delve into multi-dimensional matters, the pineal gland will become center to that research. Of all the adventures taken by humanity, those into the mental arena will be most rewarding. We only need to maintain an open mind, learning to appreciate the forthcoming endeavors. Although we have only touched on some of the pineal's potential, we will eventually unravel its full role in the spiritual evolution of humanity. Until then, we can contemplate the many possibilities.

112

CHAPTER FIVE

AWAKENING AWARENESS

For those who are interested in doing so, there are various ways to enhance psi perception and self awareness. One technique is based on attitude: simply intending to expand our consciousness will move us in that direction. However, when we do expand our awareness, the aim should not only be to reach for the highest concepts but for the WIDEST views as well. We should be careful about scoffing at new concepts. As we open our minds we allow powerful revelations to infiltrate from our Superconscious Mind, and these insights will not only be of higher caliber but of the most expansive quality we can handle.

Skeptics might protest that "seeing is believing." Yet even what we consider reality may simply be a dream in which most of us are only partially conscious. When we have third eye vision, we are able to pierce through this "hologram," viewing the real dynamism going on in Life.

As children, we have all dreamt of flying, which can be a pleasurable experience. Many theories abound to explain this phenomenon of flying. Yet the simplest answer – that we are actually flying – may turn out to be the most accurate. Of course, it is not suggested that we fly physically but that we fly with our energy bodies.

When we consciously control our dreams, we are controlling our energy bodies as well. This kind of control is known as "lucid dreaming," an ability that can be re-learned in adulthood. In such dreams, we become aware that we are actually dreaming, and this self-awareness gives us control in the dream state. Not only can we learn to consciously control our dreams but we can also visit just about any type of reality.

Information Gathering. Besides lucid dreaming, there are other techniques for visiting other dimensional realities. These methods vary from "scrying" to "astral projection" to "remote viewing" – all of which have been proven to work in their unique fashion. Any one of these three can lead to powerful insights, even mind-altering ones.

• Scrying is an ancient practice that involves perceiving past, future or distant areas. The physical tools for this practice are made of reflective or translucent substances – such as crystals, glass, mirrors or simply water. Although the most common tool is usually a crystal ball, any smooth surface will suffice. The practice has been used in many cultures through countless time as a means of divining answers to Life's questions. Depending on the culture, the forthcoming visions have been credited to either spirits, gods or even the Subconscious Mind. But whether we attempt scrying, astral projection or remote viewing, it is a very personal experience that can shake our conventional view of reality.

• Astral Projection. This is another ancient technique for viewing distant realities. Some see similarities between astral projection (AP) and out-of-body experiences (OBE). However, while subjects have reported OBEs at times of severe trauma – such as from a vehicle crash, major surgery or near-drowning – astral projection can be a controlled procedure.

In fact, every individual has a latent ability to travel astrally, for it is our birthright – a natural part of who we are as human beings; the experience is not reserved for a select few. On the other hand, AP is theoretical for those who have not experienced it personally. On the wondrous day that we project consciously for the first time, the process becomes self-evident.

• Remote Viewing (RV). This is a modern technique for collecting information across time and space. Some might compare it to scrying, except that RV was developed as a structured technique, while the former is done by natural inclination. That is, RV operates within the boundaries of established rules; whereas, natural psychics rely on their own personal rules. Thus their interpretations are often based on "feeling" targeted information. Of course, defining your own protocols does not make the results any less impressive. But the extraneous parameters in which RV is performed is meant to give it consistency and objectivity.

Because remote viewing follows strict protocols, it has been compared to being blind folded and dropped into a different place. After the "blindfold" is removed, the viewer sees things without necessarily understanding them. After many trial runs, researchers realized that "gifted" psychics were not the only ones with the ability to perceive faraway events. It is now known that anyone of average intelligence can be trained to remote view. However, because each of us processes information differently, every remote viewer will experience a session uniquely, thus contributing something new to the overall results.

The military was the first establishment to develop this technique. It was used to collect information about potential enemies – data that spies normally could not find. Gradually, through trial and error, various enhancements were added and the process was streamlined in the most extrinsic manner possible. Intuitive knowledge is organized by accurately transcribing it onto paper. Gathered information is recorded before the Conscious Mind is able to critique and contaminate it with pre-conceptions. Only after the session is finished and documented is analysis and rationalization allowed.

Although a precise definition of remote viewing can be difficult to describe, there are consistent principles that give it uniformity. The most generic definition for RV can be, "The ability to produce information while the viewer remains blind to the target." While various styles of remote viewing exist, there are two aspects common to all of them:

• On one level, RV is an objective discipline which can be consistently replicated on a regular basis.

• On another level, the technique is a process for downloading information.

Theoretically, the Superconscious Mind is the force which guides the Conscious Mind to specific targets during RV. Otherwise, there is no explanation for how the remote viewer knows how to find designated targets. The more settled the mind, the smoother the flow of information from Superconscious to Subconscious, where the information is stored. That is, RV works best when information is able to flow unobstructed through the Conscious Mind.

With RV, the subject's consciousness leaves the physical body, but there is no altered state of consciousness. On the other hand, the viewer does not simply close his or her eyes and suddenly "see" a target. Instead, a set of procedures is followed that allows the viewer to shift awareness – from the local area to another one. Although the process can be difficult to learn, any person of average intelligence can be trained to perform it. The only requirements are that the viewer be open to new possibilities and have a healthy sense of objectivity. Usually, multiple sessions of training are required before remote targets can be viewed accurately. The required RV skills include:

• objective, accurate reporting,
• the ability to focus, and
• openness to unusual facts.

Based on these skills, remote viewing was established as a scientific tool for research. Although initially financed by the military, remote viewing is now used for research by a variety of private companies and institutes.

Because RV is based on a very clear protocol outline, results are mostly valid and credible. In general, a protocol can be defined as: "a detailed plan for following an objective procedure." When RV is practiced without protocols, the viewer will project subjectively and thus the information may not be reliable. On the other hand, when individuals are properly trained under objective protocols, RV becomes a source for accurate data gathering.

Although one does not have to be a professional researcher to construct a protocol outline, there are essential factors that help validate the data gathered during remote viewing. These factors include:
• a totally blind target; the target can be almost anything of which one desires information – an object, event or person. Coordinates can be used when a target is a geographical location. When the

target is not a location, it can be cued by placing the target name, drawing or photograph in a sealed envelope.

• a "header" declaring the physical and emotional state of the viewer; this keeps the conscious mind distracted;

• no "front-loading" or clues are tolerated;

• a monitor, who does not have to be in close proximity to the viewer, but enforces the protocols. The monitor ensures that gathered information is not contaminated by judgment.

The remote viewer is trained to translate perceived information into physical words, symbols or drawings, so that it can be conveyed to others. The data must be related specifically and objectively. Not only must the conveying be based on objective observation, the viewer must remain passive, without any critiquing whatsoever. Sharing a viewed target in an objective manner is perhaps the most important step in remote viewing. What differentiates RV from natural psychic viewing or astral projection is the recording of information before the Conscious Mind can analyze and interpret it. Once a target is viewed, it should be described in written or sketch format as it is seen, without personal coloration. There must be no analysis whatsoever. Natural psychics, on the other hand, often compromise the accuracy of data by making personal interpretations. Although, this is not meant as judgement against the worth of "psychic" deciphering.

Our Traveling Consciousness. While skeptics have wondered whether the mind exists separately from the physical body, personal experiences have dismissed doubts for many individuals. Individuals who astral project often do not know exactly how they do it – but they are able to describe their experiences with specific details. The reader must use his or her own discretion on whether to believe or not. The objective here is simply to describe the realm of the human mind and its potential for traveling the endless worlds of reality. That is, you are not asked to blindly embrace this insight but to use your own innate judgment.

Because everything is based energy, our mental bodies must be re-energized on a regular basis. The etheric body, for example, serves as a condenser for absorption of subtle energy. When the physical body needs to be recharged, it usually does so during sleep, when the etheric and physical bodies move slightly out of sync. With the two bodies out of coincidence, it allows the etheric body to funnel subtle magneto-electric energy into the physical body.

When traveling to extra-dimensional realms it is done via the astral body – the intermediate body between soul and physical body. The astral body is said to be an exact counterpart of the perfect physical body but composed of subtle energy. While the material body is simply a biological machine for functioning within the 3D world, the astral body is a link to the soul. One theory maintains that the astral body encompasses the ego, through which the Conscious Mind functions as the earthly "I."

Joining the astral body to the physical body is an elastic cord, one end of which is fastened to the material body. However, the point at which it connects with the biological body has been a point of contention. Some authorities claim that the cord adheres to the solar plexus, a complex network of nerves in the abdomen. Others claim that the point of contact is at the medulla oblongata, which is the lower half of the brainstem. Still others claim that the ultimate connection is at the pineal gland. Of course, where the astral cord appears to connect and where it actually does connect can be two different situations. The astral cord might appear to connect at various locations, but it likely originates (and leaves) at the pineal gland.

The astral cord takes the appearance of a silvery tether and functions as an elastic-type structure. When traveling on very extensive trips, the cord appears as a very thin strand. However, as long as it is visible – in any shape or form, it indicates that the physical body is alive. While projecting, the physical body may appear dead, and its temperature will be close to that of hibernation. But the existence of a cord indicates that we are still connected to physical reality. This cord is comparable to the umbilical cord of a newborn baby, and when the proper time comes to leave our earthly body, the astral cord breaks off, allowing us to be "reborn" back into the astral dimension.

While descriptions of astral projection have been around since ancient times, modern researchers have been accumulating evidence regarding the process. The difficulty for modern researchers stems from the fact that they are studying something that is pure energy. Subtle energy structures are difficult to "prove." Nevertheless, there are ways to substantiate the existence of the astral body. Attempts at "extracting" the astral body of subjects under hypnosis have been successful. After a volunteer is placed in a deep hypnotic trance, and suggestions are given that the subject will leave his or her body, the process is allegedly accomplished. During the experiment, the subject is asked to pass through a screen of calcium sulphide. When this suggestion is followed, the screen glows with an added brilliance, apparently due to the proximity of the astral body. Since this experiment is consistently conclusive, it "proves" that consciousness exists separately from the physical body. In fact, astral projection is not dissimilar to the experience of "passing on"– the difference being that the astral cord remains attached during projection.

While skeptics stay busy demanding objective proof, other individuals consciously project their consciousness on a regular basis. For these individuals, the process is quite natural; their experiences are not open to debate but are their own proof. In fact, conscious astral projection is meant to be a normal process for everyone, for it is humanity's natural birthright. Allegedly, we all astral project every night when asleep, but it is done with limited consciousness. While nightly expeditions are involuntary for most, a few individuals deliberately accomplish it with full consciousness.

Whether accomplished spontaneously or deliberately, astral projecting can be an easy process for some – i.e., after the first successful attempt. The experience has been compared to the hesitation we feel before our first hang gliding experience. Similarly, one must learn control over our fears regarding astral projection. When we become self-disciplined, we are freed to visit many exciting worlds.

Mental Domains. Those who are able to consciously project their consciousness, either astrally or remotely, are free to travel throughout different realms. Sometimes they travel to alien worlds which have little similarity to our own.

While many astronomers and space engineers have focused on radio signals as a means of contacting extraterrestrial intelligences, the real key to making contact is via what is known as the subspace realm.

Astral projection and remote viewing free us from our earthly limitations. In fact, the universe is our domain to explore, and this includes different dimensional realities. The true nature of reality consists of a series of layers extending from extremely dense matter to the finest frequencies. Traveling via our consciousness is very real in every sense, except that the physical body is left behind temporarily. When we project our consciousness, there is no doubt that one is actually visiting other dimensional realms, where the reality can be very different from our own.

Some of the other realities may be populated with entities, some of which are beautiful or they may be grotesque to our senses. Some travelers have reported seeing worlds very similar to ours;

others have seen worlds inhabited by angelic or demonic beings. Of course, our perception of foreign worlds is based on our mindset – i.e., the frequency pattern of our beliefs. Not only is perception of reality based on what we project but also on what we expect. There appear to be two basic types of domains: short-lived, subjective, where we are the only inhabitant; and then there are worlds that are permanently inhabited by societies held together by their shared beliefs. In other words, we may create our own abstract world based on what we expect to see. But there also exist worlds that are as real to their inhabitants as the earth world is real to us.

One subspace realm in particular is known as the Akash. This domain is said to be the "universal library" of all knowledge – past, present, as well as probable futures. It is said that this cosmic library holds a record of everything that has ever been said or done, anywhere and everywhere in the universe. The Akash records are composed of energetic impressions. Anyone with the proper training is able to access this library, thereby learning the accurate history of the Earth. They are also able to view probable futures, perceiving a fluid future that is ever-shifting, for the future is based on the Unconscious Consensus – which refers to the shared beliefs that bind a society. These beliefs move us through our shared reality, where expectations dictate the flow of Life.

Some researchers have theorized that we do not actually travel to distant locations during astral or remote projection – but that we simply tune into other frequencies. Since we are accustomed to thinking of travel in terms of space, then we perceive our consciousness as traveling through physical domains. But the travel experiences are very real in every sense, for all experiences are simply perception of reality. One should not assume that simply because an experience exists only in the mind that it is not a valid reality – for all realities occur in the mind! The difference is that our earthly reality is more concrete and more lasting. It takes a lot of energy to create things in our reality, but once they come into existence they last much longer than they do in other realities. For example, in the dream world, things manifest and disappear according to our momentary thoughts. Since many extra-terrestrial worlds are more pliable, we must carefully control our thoughts – especially our fears. What is ironic is that, while we exist in the earth dimension, we crave changeability. But when we visit subspace realms, we crave our world of relative permanence.

Embracing Psi Consciousness. Because the ego was developed to ensure our survival in the earthly dimension, it continually works to convince us that it is a waste of time to attempt any type of psi awareness. The logic behind this argument is that psi perception does nothing to further our physical security or wealth. In this fashion our ego is determined to keep us focused on the physical plane.

Experienced individuals know that certain practices ensure projection of the astral body, but they do not necessarily know why these practices produce results. Likewise, those who practice remote viewing do not know how or why it works. How are we led to specific targets? How do we know how to retrieve specific information back to the Subconscious Mind? Again, there appears to be another consciousness assisting the remote viewing – and the evidence points to the Superconscious Mind.

Most individuals need to first experience astral projection or remote viewing before they fully accept them as real. This is the only way to personally validate the importance of these experiences. With the limited technology we presently have, only experiential evidence will suffice. The beginner must also realize that the vast majority of initial attempts at astral projection or remote viewing end in failure. Successes are rare, because the ego is very good at sabotaging such efforts.

Individuals who have an OBE experience while sleeping report that they were not fully asleep due to stress, noise or illness. Usually, they felt mentally awake but physically paralysized to a varying degree. Their descriptions give clues on what it takes to project our consciousness:
• elimination of fear;
• releasing of expectations;
• subjugation of the ego; and
• "quieting" the body.

The right state of mind is absolutely necessary for consciousness projection of any kind – astral or remote. It is like mentally balancing on a fine wire and reaching a perfectly balanced state of being. Most importantly, a settled, calm mind is required. Of course, each individual is unique, with his or her own personal angle. Some will approach the experience with joy; others will panic during their first successful projection. It seems that fear is the most common obstacle for most individuals. Yet no one has truly gotten hurt from this type of experience. Thus there should be no fear. There is no possibility of being stranded in some strange world, for the mental body always knows its way back to the body. Experienced travelers have been known to travel to very distant, alien worlds and still easily return to the earthly dimension. Others may fear that they will run into dangerous entities during their explorations. But most fears will only dampen our experiences, without any danger whatsoever. So, open up your mind to new horizons – and relax.

We must remember that, when we project our consciousness, we are still the same personality. We do not become angelic simply because we leave our physical body. Besides our personality, we also maintain an energetic connection with our body via the silver cord. At times, this cord seems to have a mind of its own: sometimes pushing our consciousness ahead, other times pulling it back.

Emotion will also push or pull the astral body, depending on the balance of positivity and negativity. As the length of the cord is extended, its diameter will decrease.

We need to remember that any reality is simply a reflection of our own thoughts and expectations. Thus, we only have to think ourselves back into our bodies – and it will happen. The fact is, it is harder to stay away from the body than it is to return to it. There has never been any evidence of anyone dying or getting harmed during their multi-dimensional explorations. Another commonly feared sensation is that of falling. This experience can be broken by simply letting ourselves go with the experience.

Desire is key, for it makes a strong impression on the Subconscious Mind as an activating factor. When desire is suppressed, it eventually leads to dreams of expression and often into real expressions. So this principle can be used consciously for our traveling endeavors. As desire for mental projection builds up, one should state, "I will project." The repetition will engrave the desire within the Subconscious Mind and will eventually move the mental body out of the physical body. This is known as passive willpower. Active willpower, on the other hand, can interfere with our attempt to project our consciousness.

It is important to not confuse desire to move the physical body with desire to project our consciousness. If we wish to mentally project, we must think of moving upwards, feeling the mental body losing it adhesion to the body. The concept would be akin to an air balloon loosing its anchors and gradually rising. Most first attempts are unsuccessful, so do not get discouraged! Beware of the ego convincing you that astral projection is a waste of time; don't let it divert your attention away from your objective. As we visualize floating above our physical body, the visualization will continue via the Subconscious Mind, as mental projection begins to take place.

It is important to keep our objective to ourselves, because talking about it with others will relieve the "stress," thereby diminishing the impetus to project. Before going to sleep every night, we should mentally hold the concept of projecting, making it a nightly routine. Be means of routine, we will gradually build up a thoughtform, so that when we do fall asleep, the thoughtform will eventually initiate the projection.

It is rare for any individual to experience 100% conscious projection during the first episode. Also, the day after a successful projection, one may feel mentally and physically tired. This is because mental projection can take a lot of energy. However, one will re-energize completely within a few days.

No specific method for projection fits everyone. On the other hand, since all experiences have a bio-chemical basis, it makes sense to assist consciousness projection via chemistry. Many sources refer to the process of mental projection by means of drugs – natural as well as artificial substances. For instance, some individuals claim to have watched their body being operated on. Inversely, it is interesting to note that there are drugs that prevent astral projection – for example, strychnine.

Certainly, the power of belief is very important to successful projection, whether astral or remote. It is thus important to fully accept that projection is possible and that we will successfully accomplish it. If we can visualize the process, we can do it!

142

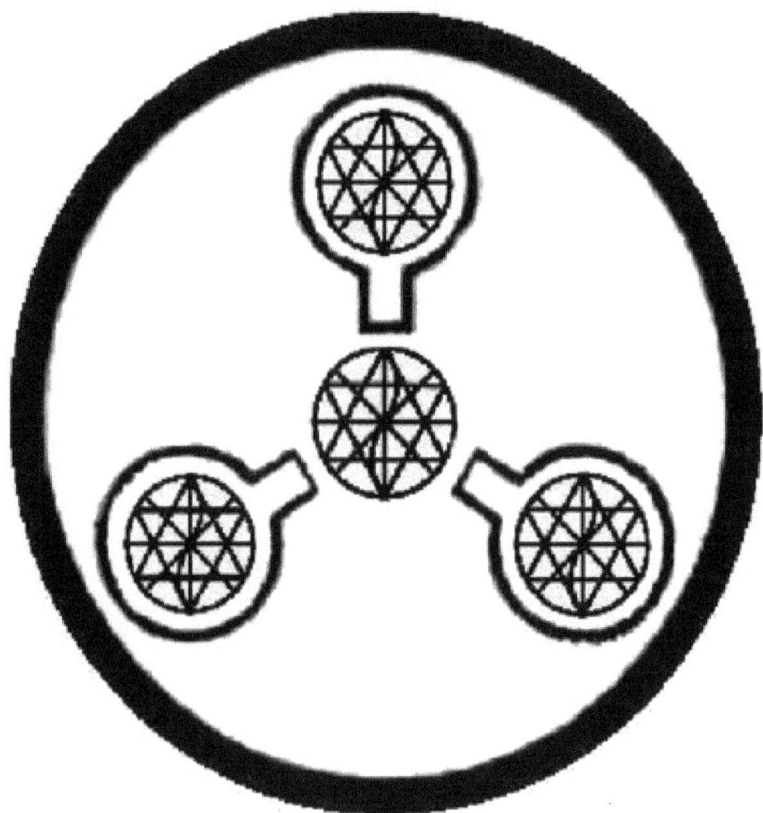

CHAPTER SIX

CHEMICAL KEYS

Using chemistry as a key to expanding consciousness is akin to tuning channels on a television. Thus researchers have sought to understand the profound effects that various substances have on human consciousness. Of course, this book does not recommend the use of illegal substances for any purpose. Rather, the point is to inform the reader of the importance of mind-altering factors in regards to the psyche. It is important to know of their existence and of their effects, because under the right circumstances, chemicals can be very constructive tools.

Many psyche influencing chemicals exist naturally throughout the world, and therefore the body is somewhat familiar with them. Some of these chemicals even occur naturally within the body. Within this framework, many ancient cultures relied on plants to increase innate perception. Their use helped them assimilate inner knowledge more readily by encouraging its application as wisely as possible.

Chemicals can also help initiate out-of-body experiences (OBEs). Some of the chemicals for this purpose are artificial; others are natural. When using artificial drugs, it is especially important to remember that smaller doses are usually most effective, since the body is not familiar with them. In fact, full anesthetic doses of any drug may produce loss of consciousness, along with a confusing state. Whereas, smaller doses are usually more than adequate to initiate an OBE.

Drugs, Chemicals & Herbs. Some of the substances known to induce a projection of consciousness include the following:

• Ayahuasca is a brew prepared mostly from the Banisteriopsis vine. This psychoactive substance is usually mixed with leaves from the Psychotria genus. Therefore ayahuasca does not refer to one single plant but to a mixture of two or more plants: it is a psychedelic combination of plants which varies in potency according to the skill of its maker. The name ayahuasca means "vine of the soul," and shamans of Western Amazonian tribes use it in religious and healing ceremonies. It is one of the most potent catalysts for expanded awareness developed by human beings.

• Salvia Divinorum – literally translated as "diviner's sage," this plant has a long tradition with shamans for facilitating visionary states of consciousness.

• Mescaline is a natural alkaloid, occurring in several cactus species, especially in Peyote (Lophophora Williamsii) and San Pedro (Trichocereus Pachanoi). In addition to containing mescaline, these cacti contain a variety of other related psychoactive compounds, helping to produce experiences that are qualitatively different than when mescaline is used alone. In ancient times mescaline's use was concentrated in Mexico, Texas and the Andes mountain region – areas where Peyote and San Pedro originally grew naturally.

Mescaline was the first psychedelic compound to be isolated and extracted. Then it became the first psychedelic to be synthesized in the laboratory. Today, American natives throughout North and South America continue to use it in conjunction with sacred traditional ceremonies. Quite frequently, it is claimed that its users embark on astral flights which take them across time and space. The ability to project astrally is allegedly enhanced when mescaline is added to other plants such as Belladonna, which can be poisonous in large doses.

• Galantamine is an alkaloid that is obtained from bulbs and flowers; it is used for memory and dream support. And thus it can increase one's odds of experiencing an OBE. Taken in small amounts (4 to 8 mg), many individuals are successful with their attempts at consciousness projection. Some claim that, coupled with choline bitartrate, it will dramatically increase a subject's odds of memory consolidation during dreaming. When used in conjunction with meditation, the success rate is increased even more. However, without proper meditation techniques, the use of galantamine will only result in a vivid dream.

• Ketamine, also known as "K," has traditionally been used in veterinary medicine. But it is also used (illegally) to induce a state of "dissociative anesthesia" within humans – producing out-of-body experiences. An OBE is usually reached with 1/10 of the amount used for anesthesia. It may be the safest of all anesthetics, since it does not suppress respiratory or gag reflexes.

• Phencyclidine - also known as Angel Dust, PCP or

Moon Dust on the street, it is often used as a recreational, dissociative drug. It exhibits hallucinogenic effects as well. Formerly used as an anesthetic agent, it is illegal to possess without government approval.

• Mimosa Hostilis (Tenuiflora) - While ayahuasca brews are produced by mixing plants that contain DMT with other plants that inhibit its breakdown in the stomach, Mimosa Hostilis can be brewed by itself. One of its compounds, Yuremamine, works in the capacity of inhibiting the breakdown of DMT.

Note: Although the aforementioned plants can be bought legally, it is illegal to purchase them specifically for their DMT content. It is an ironic angle in efforts to control mind-altering plants.

The Molecular Key. Dimethyl-tryptamine (DMT), a naturally occurring psychedelic drug, is found within many species as well as in the human body, where its exact function is still being determined. It is a relatively common molecule. The fact that it is found widespread throughout the planet's ecosystems indicates that it must play a very important role within life forms..

Not only is DMT common, but it also has very esoteric effects on the human psyche. (Interestingly, the pineal gland is geared to synthesize it as needed.) At the molecular level, it is very closely related to the fungal psilocybin and to serotonin, one of the most important neuro-transmitters in the brain. In fact, DMT, serotonin, ibogaine, LSD and psilocybin are related in that they all contain tryptamine as a basic building block.

A wide number of plants contain DMT, which is what gives ayahuasca its extra-ordinary visionary powers. Two plants rich with DMT are Prestonia Amazonia and Psychotria Viridis. The venom of the Sonora Desert Toad also contains high levels of 5-methoxy-DMT, a compound that is very closely related to human DMT.

While the brain needs a basic amount of DMT for maintaining normal brain function, levels above the average usually result in unusual experiences. Subjects who receive extra DMT experience profound revelations. Often they enter strange realms and meet exotic intelligent beings, some of which can be quite disturbing. These alternate realities are as real as our own three-dimensional world. They appear strange only because we do not perceive them during normal consciousness. Psychic travelers are convinced that they have made contact with real beings, for they are able to compare these experiences with their regular dream escapades.

Subjects often remark feeling enhanced vibrations brought on by DMT, like energy pulsating throughout their body at a higher frequency. Colors are enhanced and there is a sense of timelessness – at least as we understand the flow of time. Besides other beings, a variety of complex geometric patterns are often perceived, some of which appear Mayan, Aztec or Greek. Other common images include crystals, spinning discs and stairways. All these images point towards the existence of realities adjacent to our own. It is fascinating to ponder what these realities mean in regards to our own. Did Life develop DMT as a key for unlocking doorways to other realities? If not, it is inconceivable that such an abundant chemical would not have real importance.

And if DMT is not significant, why would the body produce it at all? Why is it one of the few natural chemicals that can cross the blood-brain barrier? And why is it found so abundantly throughout Nature? The friction between what we know intellectually and what we experience with the aid of DMT will continue until we accept that other dimensional realities exist beyond our own.

Using DMT as a key is like tuning the channel on our television set – switching our focus from everyday reality to other dimensions. It is a tool for switching consciousness to other realities. Somehow, this chemical – also known as the spirit molecule – pulls and pushes our brain chemistry beyond third dimensional awareness. It elicits psychological states that are sometimes labeled as "spiritual." In fact, it can help uncover important insights which many scientists have difficulty accepting. In this respect, it may enable us to investigate the "objective" aspects of other dimensions.

One of the problems with researching the mind has been a lack of tools. Even with DMT as a research tool, results can vary day to day and from subject to subject. For instance, one day the DMT experience may be one of ecstasy and wisdom; another day it may be one of fear and consternation. Still, the overall consensus is a feeling of undeniable certainty in the reality of the experience, however strange it may be. For investigators to appreciate the full worth of DMT as a research tool, they must first understand how it works on the brain.

Apparently, DMT affects the brain's ability to receive information. Rather than generating new perceptions, it facilitates reception of information. Somehow it allows the mind to perceive the multi-dimensional aspect of Life, pulling back the veil that normally hides alternate realms. Thus DMT acts as a key for unlocking inter-dimensional access.

Although DMT-initiated experiences challenge conservative views, eventually they will be taken more seriously. One exciting prospect is that of meeting other intelligent beings who populate other realms. Could these beings simply be figments of our imagination? Or do they exist independently of our minds? The evidence seems to indicate the latter, that they exist independently of us, just as we exist independently of their thoughts. Some of these alien beings seem very aware of humanity's existence and have indicated interaction with us throughout millennia of time. It is ironic that many serious researchers have never realized that ETs could be reached through inner space.

Instead, they have focused on giant antennae, radio signals and/or bright lights. And because the results from using external means have been null, many astronomers have concluded that we have not been visited by ETs. On the other hand, inner-space journeys have indicated otherwise.

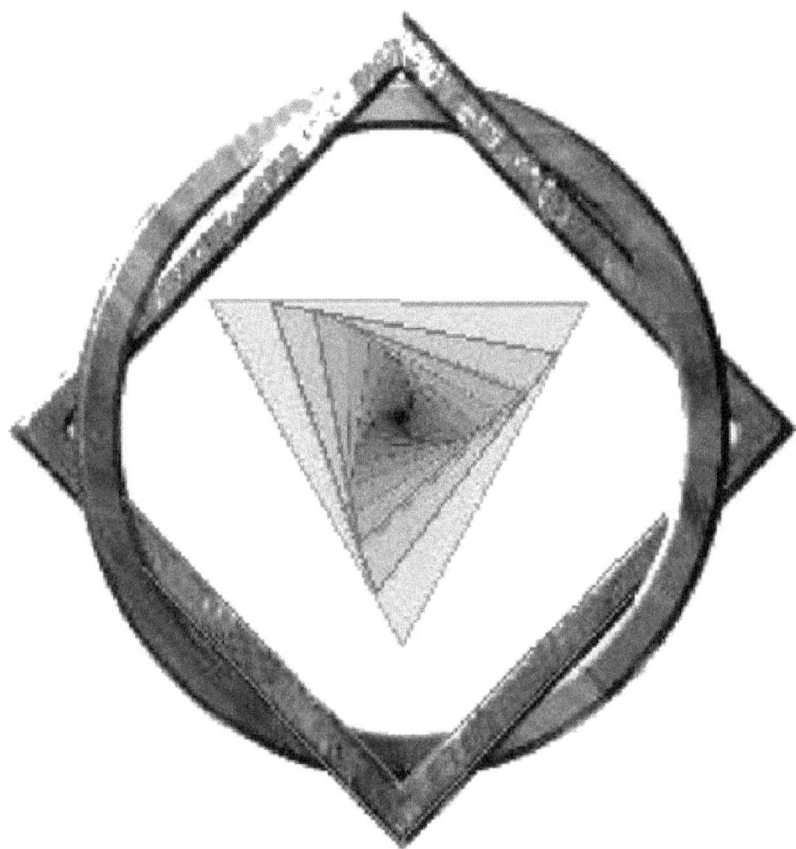

CHAPTER SEVEN

EXPANDING CONSCIOUSNESS

The state of illumination is often described as being inspired by divine light. It is a spiritual light which encourages us to make our own choices rather than embracing victimization. Ideally we should anchor personal insight with practicality, gradually aligning them with each other in the most workable fashion possible. With daily effort, our progress can be steady and sure.

Beliefs Are Switches. Beliefs are important to our progress because they are keys to the mind. We must constantly remember that beliefs follow us wherever we go, forming our daily reality. Certainly, the greatest beliefs are those that reference our personal worth. We can learn to operate our personal beliefs within the social belief structures we live in. For example, people with similar ideas naturally gravitate to each other, thus reinforcing each other's beliefs. On the other hand, if we can choose to change our beliefs, thereby moving contrary to the views of our adopted groups. However, switching gears is sometimes necessary and for the better.

Because we live in a physical world, ideas may appear surreal and lacking in power – but we should never underestimate their power! Our beliefs and thoughts have very real EM frequencies. And as is now common knowledge, EM frequencies can have powerful effects on our physical structures.

Beliefs are as fluid and energetic as weather patterns, being regulated by natural laws as are energy currents. They push and pull probabilities according to their specific patterns. Thus, when we establish new patterns of thought, our lives shift to accommodate the new frequencies. In a way, beliefs are like ghost chemicals which affect not only our physical environment but also our mental structure. However, they are more than phantoms, for they are powerful movers of energy. As representatives of our consciousness, they have real effects. For example, our imagination follows our beliefs, thereby transforming them into physical experiences.

We should integrate into our consciousness the fact that beliefs form our experiences, that they bring real effects into our lives – for they are reality in the making. Beliefs do this by collecting and holding energy patterns, which are then organized into physical structures or experiences. As we focus our consciousness on specific beliefs, we draw those things into our lives. For example, if we dwell on our limitations, we become imprisoned by those limitations. On the other hand, if we focus on the unlimited nature of reality we become empowered.

Beliefs can also be compared to furniture, for they can be moved or replaced as we choose. Our personal beliefs are ours to control; they are not meant to control us. Our perception of reality may influence our beliefs, but the most powerful understanding is that we control our reality via our beliefs – we choose what frequencies to transmit!

Software For the Mind. Every individual desires mastery over his or her life. Unfortunately, many begin their lives with enthusiasm only to gradually fall into despair. As they attempt to succeed in Life, many flounder and blindly reach for their ideals – only to end up hopelessly trapped in a rut. Unfortunately, hope gradually dies for many individuals, killing their dreams in the process.

We are not always conscious that our actions are directly related to our core beliefs – our philosophical foundation. Thus we should make a conscious effort to become cognizant of their power. We can train ourselves to become aware of particular beliefs, self-analyzing on a daily basis. Most importantly, we should be honest regarding our true selves. As we become aware of our personal belief structures, we can also modify them – thus shifting gears for the better. One way of re-structuring our beliefs is by means of affirmations (known as mantrums in ancient cultures). For example: "Every day, in every way, I get better and better." This is a classic affirmation and an excellent mantra for reprogramming the Subconscious Mind. Since every suggestion that goes into the Subconscious must first go through the Conscious Mind, we must find ways to bypass its filtering structure. Mental filters allow for only two types of beliefs:

• Those that tell us what we can do; and
• Those that tell us what we can not do.

Either type of belief can be reprogrammed by

means of constant affirmation. Once beliefs bypass the Conscious belief filter, the Subconscious does not have the ability to reject or criticize because the Submind accepts all input as truth. Through this process, we are free to be architects of our own personal future.

When false beliefs are modified for the better, the process clears channels to our Higher Mind – the Superconscious. With false beliefs cleared away, channels are opened to the wisdom and power of the Superconscious Mind. But first we must accept that we can change our belief structures; then we must accept that we should change them:

- Step One: Identify what our beliefs are.
- Step Two: Know that we can change our beliefs.
- Step Three: Accept that we should change our beliefs.
- Step Four: Practice changing our beliefs through affirmations.

For us to fully understand our belief structures we must be willing to discriminate objectively. If we are truly honest with ourselves, we will recognize many beliefs that no longer serve us. We will realize that we have embraced them simply because we have been too lazy to examine them. We will also realize that false beliefs have given us a false picture of reality.

Integration is Empowerment. Because Life tends to manifest in polarities, our perception of Life tends to be of a polar nature as well. For example, when we feel inner attitudes, we perceive those same attitudes in external conditions via projection. In reality, we are simply externalizing our feelings as outer reality. Of course, the Principle of Polarity is neither inherently bad or good – it is simply one of the precepts which moves reality.

Until we learn to master the Principle of Polarity, we continue to limp along, frequently falling off balance. For us to overcome unbalancing concepts we must harness our true beliefs, which manifest external conditions accordingly. As we become ever more conscious of our beliefs, we learn to balance all aspects of our mind. This means fully integrating our ego with our higher persona.

When we successfully integrate all segments of ourselves – beliefs, attitudes, ego, Subconscious, Conscious and Superconscious – we develop a magical equation. Ultimately it comes down to personal motivation, for books can only offer direction and inspiration. One must develop inner spiritual willpower and grace to integrate personal knowledge with our higher inspirations. In fact, any kind of success is due to a spiritual equation of energy patterns. Certainly, following others is not an inferior quality, for we can learn by following in their footsteps. But ultimately, it is important to integrate our experiences with higher aspirations, for that is the ultimate goal: to align the ego self with the Higher Self.

Integrating our total selves is a methodical process of first removing limiting beliefs and then planting new ones in their place. Mental limitations block us from perceiving a comprehensive view of the whole, causing us to perceive Life in terms of petty values. On the other hand, elimination of erroneous beliefs enables us to focus on what is truly important.

We always have a choice: to either maintain symbols of failure, or to take control of our lives with new equations. Clearly, attitude determines largely what we perceive in Life. For example, if we see only darkness and oppression, the perception will guarantee personal failure. Fear weakens us because it externalizes our energy in the form of opposition to ourselves. On the other hand, neither is a passionless life worthy of living: it denies the reason for which we manifest on the Earth – which is to explore the material world by means of our passions. Thus our lives will be fulfilled only when we follow our highest passions.

Because the ego's sole desire is to survive in the physical world, it has grown disproportionate to its original purpose. It no longer exists simply to ensure physical survival; it wishes to continue being the dominate purpose for existence. However, survival of the ego was never meant to be the purpose for human life; rather, the ego was simply created as a means for survival. And when it predominates in our decision making, it can obstruct our aspirations for greater awareness.

Ultimately, the Higher Self is the source of our passions and inspirations. And when we allow the ego to suppress our spiritual passions, we lose touch with our Higher Selves, thereby weakening our core empowerment. However, we can re-connect with our Superconscious through a two-fold process:

• On a receptive level, we must open our hearts to the power of grace, which then leads to an understanding of how all things fit in the bigger picture;

• On a proactive level, we must actively encourage a higher frequency to flow within us; essentially it simply requires that we intend it.

Without doubt, humanity has been a very industrious species, having created many wondrous things. But the next step in human evolution will be in the mental realm. And the leap will occur only when our egos allow us to do so, when we realize that there is more to Life than mere egotistical existence. We will reach this critical point when we decide that we want it more than physical wealth, that living for our spiritual passions instills a greater sense of fulfillment.

The ego's need for total control is a neurotic condition and is incompatible with higher insights. By loosening the ego's grip, we allow for the assimilation of the highest insights possible. True integration of Life is beyond the simple dynamo of acting and reacting to circumstances. As we learn to integrate our egotistical self with our Higher Self, we will uncover solutions that unlock many puzzles of Life. Higher insights will teach us that there is a higher way of living beyond simple instinct, for inspired thought is meant to guide us "to higher ground." Thus we can learn to apply our consciousness in conjunction with inspiration, for this is an equation that will lead us into greater inter-dimensional realities.

We are meant to be more than reactionary automatons. We can be more than re-actors to circumstances; we can be co-creators with Life. Our consciousness is such that we can learn to make sound judgments by applying thoughtful introspection – making decisions beyond basic reactionary impulses. The synergy of integrating our egotistical self with our Higher Self will catalyze us into a consciousness that focuses like a laser, cutting through debilitating falsehoods. Most importantly, it will allow us to develop a consciousness that perceives the entirety of Life.

As a last resort, our collective consciousness may have to be shocked into perceiving a wider reality. This will be done by individuals deliberately violating conventional rules – that is, by carrying out actions previously unheard of before. By this means, the nature of reality as previously understood will be shaken and radically transformed. Such courageous demonstrations will create cognitive dissonance, preventing narrow-minded individuals from doubting new perspectives. Since "seeing is believing," the assumed order of things will have no choice but to bend to a new reality. However, shock therapy will only be a last resort, for there is already a growing number of individuals who are gradually shifting our collective perception for the better.

To pierce collective reality as it is now, a critical mass must first be reached. Enough individuals (1/10th of 1%) must be convinced of their self worth and encouraged to jump out of their mental boxes. Shifting global reality means first changing ourselves, which then leads to a paradigm shift. In other words, changing social reality is secondary to taking mastery over our personal lives, for we change collective reality by first changing our individual attitudes.

Manifestation, Our Legacy. Humanity is coming to a crossroads where it will be required to shift its paradigm of thinking. It is the author's hope that the reader will join countless others who are awakening to this shift. But humanity will be catapulted into a bright future only when enough individuals come to acknowledge their personal power and responsibility.

The power to manifest our dreams is our birthright. However, we are required to actively claim this power; the alternative is to simply wallow in self-pity. Blaming Life for our misfortune will never lead to happiness. Instead, we can develop an empowering consciousness based on the integration of the ego and Higher Self.

Our personal endeavors are ours alone to decide, but they require our focused willpower and grace. Not only must we know what we truly desire, but we must also accept that we deserve them. If we can imagine our objectives, we can accept their validity. Furthermore, we must be willing to physically invest action beyond visualization. In other words, we must be willing to personally invest in our dreams. These factors may seem like common sense – and they are! But we need constant reminding, for we all get caught up in the complexity of egotistical drama.

When we live our lives with purpose, the result is joy and hope for the future. It is a hope that always keeps our consciousness open to new views, insights and angles. It is not blind hope – rather, it is one filled with knowing and determination. This attitude then leads to a catalytic implosion, which occurs only when we are willing to integrate hope with our highest aspirations.

Individuals who embrace higher views are "rallying points" for others wishing to embrace the same ideals. They are sparks of light that awaken others to their power and potential. By this means, they help push beyond the walls of conventional reality, leading us into a higher, more enriching realm.

BIBLIOGRAPHY
& RECOMMENDED READING

Arjuna. *The Single Eye.* 1921

Brown, Courtney (PhD). *Cosmic Voyage.* 1996

Hancock, Graham. *Supernatural: Meetings with the Ancient Teachers of Mankind.* 2007

Ireland, Richard. *The Phoenix Oracle.* 1970

Magnus, John. *Astral Projection: And the Nature of Reality.* 2005

McMoneagle, Joseph. *Remote Viewing Secrets: A Handbook.* 2000

Muldoon, Sylvan & Hereward Carrington. *The Projection of the Astral Body.* 1982

Powers, Melvin. *Self Hypnosis: Its Theory, Technique and Application.* 1956

Rampa, T. Lobsang. *The Third Eye.* 1958

Sonero, Devi. *Secrets of Hypnotism.* 1970

Strassman, Rick (MD). *DMT: The Spirit Molecule.* 2001

Strassman, Rick (MD) et al. *Inner Paths to Outer Space.* 2008

Turner, D.M. *The Essential Psychedelic Guide.* 1994

178

9 780962 168277